creative ESSENTIALS

Kate!
here it is...
thanks for
all your
brilliant
inspiring
contributions
with love
Lucy
X

Lucy Scher

READING SCREENPLAYS
how to analyse and evaluate film scripts

creative ESSENTIALS

First published in 2011 by Kamera Books,
an imprint of Oldcastle Books
PO Box 394, Harpenden, Herts, AL5 1XJ
www.kamerabooks.com

Copyright © Lucy Scher 2011
Series Editor: Hannah Patterson

978-1-84243-510-6 (print)
978-1-84243-511-3 (kindle)
978-1-84243-512-0 (epub)
978-1-84243-513-7 (pdf)

2 4 6 8 10 9 7 5 3 1

Typeset by Elsa Mathern
Printed and bound by Clays Ltd, St Ives plc

ACKNOWLEDGEMENTS

The Script Factory's Reader Training (and related) courses have been taught by Justine Hart, Marilyn Milgrom, Ludo Smolski, Rob Ritchie, Angeli Macfarlane, Kate Leys, Jonny Brown, Tracy O'Riordan, Sarah Harper-Barnes and Ranald Allan. Special thanks to Angeli Macfarlane, who I worked with on the Pathe Prize, selecting three projects out of some 2,000 submissions for a Script Factory reading. This greatly accelerated my learning and expertise in teaching script reading.

My thanks to...
Alexandra Wilds for allowing me to report on her script *Broken Heart Boot Camp*; Peter Scher, my dad, who read the material and ensured it made sense; my mum, Anne Scher; my editor, Hannah Patterson, for asking me to do it, and Anne Hudson for her invaluable contributions along the way; my co-director of 11 happy years, Briony Hanson, now Director of Film for the British Council; and Sheena Bucktowonsing, our company manager these last two years. Together with Justine Hart, current co-director, Briony and Sheena shared their passion for film and encouraged this writing endeavour with much support and good humour. And my huge personal thanks go to Clare Muller for everything else.

Finally, my thanks to Charlotte Macleod for taking a punt on me in 1996 and letting me join her to launch The Script Factory.

CONTENTS

INTRODUCTION

Script readers are crucial to the film industry, often responsible for determining whether a script is even looked at by a producer or development executive. Yet those accountable for reading scripts are often on the first rung of the industry ladder and, even when they are already working in the film world, may have had little or no training for the task. This book is based upon knowledge acquired during the years of teaching the Script Factory Reader Training Course both in the UK and internationally. The course has used good produced scripts as well as a huge range of unproduced projects, very generously made available by aspiring screenwriters. Participants have ranged from heads of studios, heads of funds and screen agencies, producers, distributors, commissioners, directors, agents and screenwriters, as well as those seeking to start a career in reading and development. The intention of this book is to equip *anyone* who reads (or indeed writes) scripts and is required to make some judgement upon them, whatever their role and experience in the wider film industry, with the confidence and skills to write intelligent, informed script reports.

Scripts are usually first read at a very early stage of a film's development. Every filmmaker will tell you that the story will continue to be rewritten dozens of times, both before and during production, and won't be completed until the final edit. The job of the reader, therefore, is not to judge a fledgling film script against acclaimed movies but rather to discern whether there is enough potential in the idea to make it worth the writer's time and effort, or the producer's cash, to invest in another draft that might eventually be shaped into a film.

For the past 13 years the Script Factory has been training readers to read screenplays a little more generously; not to suggest that something is good when it clearly isn't, but rather not to dismiss a good idea that may currently be let down by simplistic characterisation or a weak structure, things that could be fixed through wise development and honing of the writer's craft. A skilful script reader should be able to see past such weaknesses and glimpse what the finished film could be if the writer's intentions were to be successfully realised.

Alongside the chapters on the detail of the script report, including a sample report, this book incorporates an analysis of genre and how to use it in reading and development; a chapter on both writing and assessing treatments; and a final section on the job of development, both what it is and how to manage the transition from reading scripts to working with screenwriters.

Understanding how a script is assessed and developed is possibly the most valuable training that a screenwriter can access and, if you read this as a writer, the step-by-step process of analysing the material offers you the best way to obtain distance from, and objectivity about, your project to help in making the decisions that will improve it.

I joined the newly conceived Script Factory to produce the first season of screenplay readings in the autumn of 1996. Our aim was to showcase the scripts of the UK's finest screenwriters and bring them to life with exceptional actors, in front of a film-industry audience, to celebrate the craft of writing for the screen.

My work involved reading each of the scripts, at least twice, and then listening to them being delivered by actors at a tempo that enabled me to visualise the action. In this way, and entirely unexpectedly, I learned the craft of screenplay. It was an enormously privileged, and perhaps unique, start to a development career.

I only became aware that I had acquired this skill when the Script Factory project opened its doors and I began to read scripts by hopeful and enthusiastic new writers who clearly didn't know or understand the craft of screenwriting. In an effort to convey some of the knowledge that I had absorbed I wrote script reports, first on an ad-hoc basis to anyone who asked, and then launched the Script Report Service that still runs today. This offers any screenwriter a constructive, analytical report on their project to help them decide the development priorities for the next draft.

The success of the Script Report Service created the need for more readers than just myself. The ones available at that time wrote 'coverage' for executives, and had a style that was personal, but often very critical and inappropriate to offer the writer. As I had paid work to offer to successful participants, in the summer of 1999 I felt confident enough to launch a Report Writing Course. I devised some exercises and processed the learning I had absorbed about story and screenwriting craft into six lecture sessions.

Over the years the report-writing course and its content has been developed and refined, improved and expanded and I am indebted to all the trainers for their invaluable contributions. And, of course, we have gained immeasurably from the many thousands of participants who have taken part and warmly and generously offered their insights, thoughts and experiences. However, my debt is greatest to my Script Factory co-director Justine Hart who brought extraordinary intellectual rigour to the material; much of the thinking and precision about how to convey it in this book are hers.

Our hope is that this book conveys to you the spirit of the course as well as the detail, and remains an inspiring and relevant companion throughout your career.

1. STORYTELLING AND THE PRINCIPLES OF GENRE

Reading screenplays requires the skills to analyse the ability of the writer, first, to tell a story, and, second, to tell that story *dramatically*. This book offers a method that enables the script reader to be precise and helpful in preparing the report. But before we get to the detail of the script report, first an exploration of genre. Screenplays are incredibly textured documents and extremely hard to write. As we are reading a script, especially first or early drafts, we begin to feel gaps in the story. We start thinking about ways to fill those gaps by improving the set up, or changing the characters, or making the problems more difficult – or, indeed, simpler – or altering the outcome so the script delivers a more satisfying story. In doing this we are bringing to it a very comprehensive understanding of genre.

GENRE

Genre is a well-established technical term in the film industry. Genre categorises the type or the style of story. Genre is routinely used in marketing films, e.g. a *thriller*, a *horror*, a *romantic comedy*, a *heist*, a *gangster* film, etc. However, we use genre in script reading or development to delve beneath the surface to see the basic pattern of the story – the thriller or horror or romantic comedy, etc – that we are recognising or unconsciously beginning to understand.

We recognise the emotional territory within which the story works and the conventions used in the storytelling. Consciously using this knowledge in our thinking about the script will ensure that the analysis in the script report has relevance to industry and audience as well as the writer.

I can illustrate this from my experience in running a workshop in Macedonia for new filmmakers. I asked the class to read the local paper and pick out a story that they thought would make a good film. Every single one of them chose the same article whose headline translated as: '200 Macedonian students are to be given the opportunity to work in Disneyworld, Florida for the summer to improve their English and their relations.'

Nine students in three groups of three set about writing film versions of stories this headline suggested to them.

1. The first story presented was a comedy-drama centred around a guy aged 30. Although too old to be a student he was in love with the Disney characters, and the story related his efforts to get enrolled in a college so that he could go on the trip and meet Mickey Mouse. By the time he has succeeded and arrives in Florida, a real person has filled the gap in his life and he no longer needs Mickey.

2. The second story was a slasher film set in Disneyworld where a group of six Macedonian students is employed on the night watch when a Disney character starts to come to life. One by one the students are slaughtered until one lone girl remains, fighting for her life. In the

morning she is found alive at the top of Big Thunder Mountain, mute and unable to explain what happened. As she is returned to Macedonia and starts talking on her cell phone about collecting her friends' wages for them, the audience realises it was she who killed the others!

3. The third story was a road movie about a Macedonian Grandma who has learnt that she is dying. She decides to visit her grandson who is working in Disneyworld for the summer. She has never left Macedonia before and deeply distrusts all Americans but she obtains a visa and a plane ticket and arrives in Los Angeles; she has, of course, gone to the wrong Disney theme park. Thus begins her trip from LA to Florida, with time running out. The trip enables her to discover the commonality and humanity of all people, including Americans, at a time, and in a strange new place, when she needs it most. She arrives in time to say goodbye.

This ability to sit down in a group and quickly establish the meaning and the main character of a story and then to fill in the events which link it all up is quite extraordinary.

Stories offer a stabilising integrity and the stories that endure are those that embody clear meanings. In each of the three Macedonian student stories, the writers employed a meaningful and resonant idea, and then found a way of telling it, so that the meaning is communicated to you when you read it.

Genre provides a framework within which to structure the analysis of a script. Establishing the kind of story that the writer is writing, or aspiring to write, is fundamental. It will enable the reader to understand what the story should mean, *why* it should mean that, and how that meaning is established through the choice of character/s and events.

Be in no doubt that wherever the idea for the story originates – whether from personal experience, a newspaper article, an intriguing situation, or whatever – the reason the writer has chosen it is because it has meaning that is in some way important to the writer. The task of script reading and script development is to find that meaning and assist the writer in conveying it as effectively as possible to the audience. Absolutely essential for doing this well is for the reader to have a thorough and conscious understanding of *genre*.

FILM GENRES

There are, and always will be, many exceptions raised to all the points discussed in relation to film, storytelling and genres. The purpose of any discussion about genre is not to find unity and precise definitions but to identify and understand the various emotional territories that stories inhabit. This enables the reader to make an informed judgement about a script – the work that is needed to enhance both it and its potential to find an audience.

Film genres may be loosely divided into the two main types. They are (1) stories that deal in transgression where someone or something has upset the order of the world and the purpose of the story is to restore it, and (2) stories that deal in relationships – some of which may involve transgression but in which our interest is more likely to be in the characters rather than the outcome of the transgression.

To clarify this, consider the horror genre. This genre covers such a wide range of stories that it is impossible to define any core conventions beyond the fact that it deals in our fear of the supernatural, with the *method* of storytelling employed to deliver some visceral shocks to the audience. Thus, as a genre, it embraces stories that deal with death and grief like *The Orphanage* and *The Sixth Sense*, cave-dwelling monsters like *The Descent*, as well as *Nightmare on Elm Street* and *The Omen*.

Whilst there are some films that are clearly conceived as horror films, ones with weird children all born on a particular day (6th of June) who are evil, other stories can be seen to 'use' the horror genre to give a big-screen presence to a story idea that, if rendered as a drama, would be boring.

The Orphanage is essentially about a mother who doesn't pay proper attention to her child, who then goes missing. It's about maternal guilt and the ghosts of orphaned or lost children searching for the mothers they never had. By the end of the film, you realise that, strictly speaking, there is no malevolent force, the ghosts are just children looking for their friends, but the film still contains really creepy moments, with doors closing inexplicably and blood trickling down the walls. Consequently the audience experiences the thrills of the horror film and arguably the filmmakers have obtained a much bigger audience for a story about grief.

In assessing and analysing horror screenplays a good script reader should know that the genre is defined by its method of storytelling, and that it can encompass 'natural' grief as well as supernatural evil. This demonstrates an intelligent rather than a prescriptive approach to genre.

GENRE CONVENTIONS – EXAMPLES

When trying to apply the conventions of a genre it can be useful for the reader to structure the assessment around the building blocks of the story. For example, pose questions about the nature of the main character. What kinds of character traits are we expecting? Does the character have a goal or does the audience supply it? Do the characters change? How is the character's conflict most prominently manifested? Is the conflict internal, situational or interpersonal? What resolution are we expecting?

Here are some examples of common genres and the particular considerations each presents for the script reader.

Rites of passage

It is common for writers, and even readers, to classify any story in which a young person learns something as a rites of passage story, but this is not always the case. The term 'rite of passage' applies to an event or ceremony that marks the transition from one recognisable stage of life to the next. Our present culture doesn't always offer clear milestones or markers. Indeed the distinctions between the different phases of life have been blurred – a mid-life crisis can occur in your twenties and middle age is now (happily) middle youth. However, we still recognise the phases through which we pass: childhood to adolescence; adolescence to adulthood; single to married; child-free to parenthood; working to retired.

Because film stories deal in conflict, celebrating successful transition is not usually seen in the rites of passage genre. Rather, the stories most commonly deal with characters who must struggle to make the transition – characters who are on the threshold of the next phase of life but aren't ready. Either the characters are trying to fly too soon, or life is about to require something of them that they don't yet feel equipped to give, or else circumstances will take away from them something they are not ready to surrender.

Bear in mind that the important genre convention is that the point of the story is to get the character successfully to pass through to the next phase (at the appropriate time); but this is not necessarily the goal of the character. The writer may make the character want something else or may have them resisting the transition in order to generate drama. It is the audience that cares whether or not the rite of passage is negotiated successfully. If you are reading this kind of script, analyse carefully how the writer has made us care, or what might be done to further this? The conflict for the character is internal and often situational, set by the constraints of their environment, and this conflict is manifested in problems with people such as parents, siblings, partners, etc. The character is changed by these experiences at the end of the story.

Stand By Me is still the classic 'childhood to adolescence' and 'loss of innocence' story retold from the perspective of the adult looking back; *My Life As A Dog* tells the same story from the point of view of 12-year-old Ingemar, who has to grow up very fast. *Somersault* and *An Education* both offer versions of trying to 'fly too soon' into adulthood; *Lars and the Real Girl* tells the same story but through the experiences of Lars, who hasn't made the transition to adulthood at the age of 27 and needs to. At the heart of *American Beauty* is Lester's mid-life crisis and the story is about his need to accept the stage of life he is in. *About Schmidt* is an example of the rite of passage to retirement and the recalibration of one's sense of self at this stage.

Road movie

The most important element in the road movie must be the journey, and reading a script for a road movie should reveal very clearly the motivation for undertaking it. The motive may be the desire to get away from something (the police, a boring environment) or to get to something (a beauty pageant, a sporting event) but, whatever it is, the journey should be challenging and testing for the character and it should result in change to one or more characters. The audience and the characters will share the dramatic goal of completing the journey.

Unlike many genres, the road movie can support an episodic structure; the characters journey though the story-world and the writer doesn't have the usual imperative to set up or resolve every event along the way. Whilst a single character can undertake a journey, having two or more characters on the road will contain a relationship in a physical space that can generate tension, meltdown and resolution to this story element.

In *Little Miss Sunshine*, the beauty pageant could have been set in Albuquerque, where the family lives, as there is no inherent story reason for it to be set in California. But this is a story in which the family needs to change its attitude to what it means to win. Having a van with a sticky gearshift and a broken horn effectively assists this in several ways: it keeps the family in one place whilst generating urgency and moving the story on; it gives them something to work at together every time they stop or start; it is the cause of significant practical obstacles to progress on the journey that they need to complete within a fixed time; it is absurdly unfortunate and therefore very funny; and, lastly, but still importantly, the bright yellow VW van creates a striking visual image.

There are many classic road movies (and many good books dedicated to analysing and appreciating the genre) like *Thelma and Louise*, *Bonnie and Clyde*, *Easy Rider*, *Wild at Heart*, *Mad Max*, *Fear and Loathing in Las Vegas*, *Paris, Texas*, and, more recently, *Sideways*, *Broken Flowers* and *Little Miss Sunshine*. David Lynch's *The Straight Story* is a beautiful example of the genre, telling a simple, moving story about the efforts of Alvin Straight to get to his dying brother before it is too late.

Thriller

Like horror, this is a very broad genre, but a key generic definer is that thrillers are designed to be realistic. However extreme the situation, we are aware that psychos exist and bad things do happen, and that, occasionally, we may each put ourselves in some danger. One of the most important ways that thriller stories attain realism is through the construction of the antagonist – the character who perpetrates the threat. It is imperative that the audience glimpses the motive that drives them and in such a way that, for a moment, we understand their need for revenge, justice, vengeance. The most important aspect of the protagonist, the character who is under threat, is their survival! The audience is invested in their ability to survive. The range of situations found in thriller stories is too extensive for generalisation but one consistent element is the stake. In a thriller, life is at stake. If you are reading a thriller script, ensure that the threat is to life, rather than a job, or status, or a marriage.

Beyond that inviolable principle, examine the way that an audience is involved in, and relates to, the story. In a thriller film it is through the character of the protagonist. There is no better way of describing this character than by specifying that they need to be just like us, which we may loosely define as being 'normal'. Normal people don't have too much or too little of anything. We generally have homes, families, jobs, hobbies and are generally pleasant. At the start of the story it is quite likely that the protagonist's only goal is for everything to stay as it is. These are not characters that are looking for change and, because they are not really engaged with the idea of change, they often remain quite oblivious to what is going on around them until very late in the story.

Because the story will require them to deal with a big problem, they should be invested with the right attributes such as competence, cleverness, being fit and resourceful. Any serious gaps in their functionality, like having narcolepsy or being too chubby, or a serious shortcoming that the protagonist cannot just miraculously 'overcome' in order to win through, will affect our willingness to identify with them. It is an important convention that this character isn't fundamentally changed by the experiences of the story.

There is an exception when the writer intends the thriller story also to be a cautionary tale. In this case the character can have too much of something or gaps in functionality – the character may be overly ambitious, for example, or an alcoholic.

Thriller stories can also rely on dramatic irony, on the audience having more information about the situation than the character/s, and in this way the story can elicit our care and concern as well as generating the tension.

Examples of classic thriller films are *Single White Female*, *The Hand That Rocks the Cradle* and *Pacific Heights*, all of which employ the convention of dramatic irony whereby the audience knows much more than the characters. *Misery* and *Fatal Attraction* both offer a masterclass in generating tension with the premise of crossing paths with the wrong person and the danger of misreading the signs. More recently, good thriller films have included *Internal Affairs*, *The Departed*, *State of Play* and *Tell No One*.

Romantic comedies

Audiences enjoy romantic comedies, obtaining a vicarious experience of the power of love and confirmation of the ideal that 'the one' exists. Attaining this should be the main objective of the rom-com. There is, or should be, nothing else at stake. The world depicted is benign and 'feel-good' and the rom-com's banter and situations need to be imbued with genuine and clever comedy. Over the last ten years or so the romantic comedy genre has evolved from being the exclusive preserve of the young, straight, white middle classes. The protagonists may now be old, black, gay, religious, ugly, and so on. What remains common to the stories is the controlling idea that 'the one' exists for the protagonists and that, of course, the protagonists are entitled to experience and consummate this love.

This entertainment is not hard to sell to an audience. We all believe that everyone deserves to love and be loved so the task of the writer is to convey this underlying 'truth' through the characters. The job of the reader is to ascertain that this has been done convincingly, particularly in rom-coms where the characters display seemingly unpleasant characteristics such as arrogance, smugness, presumption or vanity.

Consider where, and how effective, is the scene or sequence that enables the audience to get behind the lovers and want them to be together in the end.

A common problem in romantic comedy scripts is for one or both of the characters to be destined to learn something about themselves and to need to change in order to find the love that has eluded them so far. However the character trait or the lesson learned has to elicit the audience's empathy rather than feelings of pity, sympathy, or, worse, contempt. The character having to learn not to be a 'door-mat' is likely to be rather needy or foolish, which may well elicit sympathy from the audience, whereas the character who learns to accept him/herself as 'good enough' will be more likely to generate empathy.

It is surprisingly easy for writers to write unsatisfactory characters in a rom-com by misunderstanding the nature of the journey for both the characters and the audience.

Classic examples of romantic comedies are *When Harry Met Sally*, *Pretty Woman*, *Sleepless in Seattle*, *Four Weddings and a Funeral*, *Bridget Jones's Diary* and *Notting Hill*. More recently the genre has tackled unexpected pregnancy, deportation and splitting up rather than getting together in films like *Knocked Up*, *The Proposal*, *The Break Up* and *(500) Days of Summer*.

Drama stories

What are the conventions of the drama genre? An agreed definition is unlikely but, in my work, I find it useful to characterise dramas as stories about 'things that can happen to us'. These are things like accidents, an unwanted pregnancy, an affair, a divorce, sudden death, the suicide of someone we know, being made redundant, loss of fortune, crisis of confidence, house repossession. These events are imaginable and would impact on our lives, which we work hard to keep as ordered as possible.

Essentially, drama stories are about interruptions to life, so the drama's premise is 'life is fragile', while the meaning is simply to affirm for us that, whatever happens, 'life goes on'.

To some extent, most story ideas may be described as dramas – perhaps not highly motivated political thrillers, or murders, because they can be specific to the particulars of the story-world and characters – but most other stories tell of an interruption to someone's ordered routine, their ordinary life, whether they meet someone they are going to fall in love with or whether they are lost and can't find their way home. If a story idea can be deployed in a genre with more marketing muscle than the drama genre, suggesting that the project is steered accordingly could be the sensible approach.

Drama stories are structured around an interruption to the lives of their characters. Clearly it is important for the reader/viewer to have knowledge of life preceding the event in order to properly gauge the event's impact, and the way in which that information is delivered and managed will dictate the structure. We may come into the story long after the interruption has happened, as is the case in *Rachel Getting Married*. In this story, Kym, Rachel's sister, was 16, high on drugs and in charge of their little brother, Ethan, when she crashed the car and he died. However, the story starts some years later when Kym is out of rehab and a guest at her sister's wedding, for this is the moment when Kym is going to confront her past and find some kind of peace and resolution. The audience are aware that something happened but do not know the details until quite late in the story. *You Can Count On Me* offers a prologue. In four short scenes at the start of the film we see a couple in their car, on a winding road in heavy rain. We hear a horn blast and the crash and then cut to the local policeman ringing a doorbell that same rainy night, opened by a teenage babysitter. In the house, in the background, are two young children. The next scene is the funeral where we see two coffins and the two children holding hands tightly. The image mixes to two grave stones, and the woman tending them was that young girl. In this way the writer has told us the important information that we need in order to imbue with more depth the specific situations of the characters. In *Juno*, the interruption is integral to the story on screen. Juno's situation at the start of the story is 'pregnant' and the story explores her efforts to manage her situation.

The writer's choice of structure and how the information about the interruption is delivered will determine the specific dramatic question – the particular aspect of life that this story is concerned with. It is really important that drama stories do not try to cover all aspects of the characters' lives but offer a specific reason for this story to be told now. The dramatic question is covered in more detail in the section on structure, but, as an example, Juno's decision to give her baby to the perfect family is what drives the story, whereas the dramatic question is, 'Will Juno survive this interruption to her life and get back to being a teenager?'

There should be at least three key characters in a drama story simply because drama explores the fallout from unexpected events and characters must display a range of different reactions. Within every group there will be, at one end of the spectrum, the ones who feel cursed and unlucky and, at the other end, the ones who pick up the pieces and think it could have been worse. For a drama story to reach the broadest possible audience it should have a range of points of view, expressed through the characters, enabling each member of the audience to relate to someone on screen for some of the time at least.

Characters in drama stories do not need *specific goals*, by which I mean the passion to get into ballet school (*Billy Elliot*), or trying to bring justice to a community damaged by a negligent water company (*Erin Brockovich*). It is important that the characters are established as people getting on with their lives, simply because something is going to happen that will interrupt the normal course of events. As illustrated in the examples of *Rachel Getting Married* or *You Can Count On Me*, the characters may continue to deal with the interruption for years, but, before it happened, they were getting on with their lives. Goals may arise from the interrupting event and how it is managed (or not managed), but characters with a very specific desire or a driving passion for something may reduce the story's appeal to a broad audience. Some characters may change as a result of the experiences of the story and some may not, just like life.

The source of conflict in a drama will always be the situation which affects the characters, which is then reinforced and expressed through the relationships on screen. Unlike most other genres, drama is the one where the story may not necessarily be resolved. Life goes on. The relationships may have shifted, the worldview is a little different, nothing will be the same again, but life goes on.

Reading drama scripts requires an appreciation of subtlety in the story. To focus on the goals of the characters in the drama by trying to answer the question *what happens if the character doesn't get or achieve 'it'?* (whatever it may be) is the likeliest way to miss this subtlety. Whilst this question is usually appropriate for genre stories with a clear goal or desired outcome, in drama stories it is more important to assess whether the characters' range of responses to the event in the story feels truthful. Whether or not members of the audience have themselves experienced an unwanted pregnancy, or a redundancy, or a fatal traffic accident involving their own family, we can recognise the kinds of responses that will arise and the behaviour that will result. If the audience can understand the decisions and the actions that the characters are taking they can anticipate the outcome – good, bad, or both. Once there is an outcome to anticipate there is a story in which the audience becomes engaged. Without consequences, it may be just an account of an event.

Examples of drama films are *Kramer vs Kramer*, which tells the story of a marriage separation; *The Big Chill*, which looks at the impact of one member's suicide on a group of former college friends; and *One Night Stand*, which deals with the consequences of just that. *In the Bedroom* is a classic example of someone being in the wrong place at the wrong time and the terrible aftermath for his family. *Three Colours Blue* and *The Ice Storm* tell of accidental death; *Crash*, *27 Grams* and *Amores Perros* all look at the impact of a car crash on a range of characters.

ASSESSING STORY AND GENRE FOR THE REPORT

When you finish the first reading of a script consider carefully the genre this story belongs in (or could belong in) and use the conventions of that genre to guide your thoughts by considering these questions:

- Does it sit in the right emotional territory?
- Does the story's meaning succeed within the genre?
- Are the characters' goals appropriate to the genre? Or do they have goals not required by the story?
- Do the characters have the right attributes for the story?
- Do the characters feel truthful?

This approach is not put forward as a prescriptive one for any specific story choices in terms of the events; it should, however, help to determine that the 'component parts' which an audience may readily recognise are in place, and, in this way, the audience – both the reader and the eventual viewers – may trust that they are in good hands.

Clearly, any generic conventions may be played with or indeed ignored. This may work if there is adequate and thoughtful compensation, such that our expectations of the story are fulfilled but not in the exact way that we may be anticipate. Genre is not a method that should result in making films formulaic. Genre is about understanding that films are integral to our storytelling tradition and we all need stories to help us make sense of our lives.

Finally, script readers must trust in their understanding of how all stories work. Enjoy the learning and the thinking and be confident.

2. SCRIPT REPORT WRITING

WHAT KIND OF REPORT ARE YOU WRITING?

As a reader you will generally be required to write reports with one of two very different objectives in mind:

Either

- to evaluate the project for a development executive, producer or a commission that provides funding for script development

Or

- to offer a constructive and helpful critique of the project for the writer and possibly also the team that is developing the script

In the former case, what is required will vary from company to company but it will generally be short and to the point: a synopsis, some comments on the strengths and weaknesses of the project, a recommendation for further action (pass, second read, etc).

This type of report is often referred to as 'coverage' and allows the company executive to make an informed decision quickly about whether to pursue the project.

If, however, you are writing a report for the writer with the intention of helping them to develop their project, then you will need to write in more detail and in a way that is less critical and more analytical. This is the type of report that this book is geared towards. The reason for this is a wholehearted desire to promote the creation of script reports that offer considered and quality analysis. And once you have mastered the art of writing a report directly for the writer, any form of script analysis, regardless of its purpose, will be within your reach.

The way we encourage you to think about the script will provide you with a framework within which to structure your subjective responses, and to turn what is initially 'just a feeling' into a proper analysis of what is or isn't working. Inevitably, this will make you a more discerning reader, more confident about your own judgement, and therefore more useful to potential employers. We aim to banish the banter that characterises pub talk about films; everyone thinks they are an expert on scripts because they have seen so many films. You, on the other hand, will enjoy learning that it is an artistic and technical process that you can analyse with an expert voice.

If you are hoping to progress to work in development (or if that is where you are now and you are looking to hone your skills) this analytical approach will also lay the foundations for a constructive way of working more closely with a writer to develop their script. On the whole, script reports don't offer too many suggestions on how to improve a script; this is always a delicate area, best left for situations where you have direct contact with the writer so that suggestions can be delivered as part of a dialogue. For the purposes of the script report, a good analysis will give sufficient food for thought and enough guidance to help a writer reach certain useful conclusions on their own.

EQUIPPING YOURSELF TO READ

Script reading demands skills and knowledge: the skills bit is what we aim to dispense with this book; the knowledge is something you need to acquire through your own efforts. It is imperative that you familiarise yourself with the UK and international film industries and have a broad knowledge of cinema in general, past and present. It is crucial to love both reading and writing – you will be doing plenty of both. It helps to have a strong interest in the written word and to seek excellence in your own writing. Connection to all current cultural events is a real plus, as many films are drawn from contemporary culture: theatre, books, music and real-life events.

An empathy for a writer's intentions is one of the key skills you will bring to your work. Script reading is not in itself a proper career as it is badly paid and often sporadic work. But scripts are the blueprint of every film and the broader your understanding of how they work, the more useful you will be in any aspect of film production.

SETTLING DOWN TO READ

Here are some tips to help you get the job done effectively and efficiently:

- Read the script at one uninterrupted sitting. This will help you to 'run the movie in your head'.

- However tempting, make sure that you don't just read the dialogue. Read at a pace that enables you to form a visual image of the action in your mind. This means don't ignore scene headings, and read the scene directions. If you don't know where the characters are, it's hard to imagine the action.

- Write your report soon after reading the script – clearly, the longer you leave it, the less sharp your observations will become.

- Don't try to write your report as you go but do keep notes, with page numbers, while you are reading. This will help you to quote specific examples to support the observations you make in your report. Don't forget to note successful and enjoyable parts of the script too. A writer is more likely to take on board your criticism if praise is also offered where it is due.

- Disregard inconsequential details – typos, misspellings, grammatical errors and incorrect format – unless these make the story unintelligible or unless the script is terribly bad in more important ways. In these cases mention the technical errors in your report to add weight to the overall comment.

WRITING YOUR REPORT

Unfortunately there isn't a standard report adopted by the entire film industry, though the categories we use in our reports are fairly universal. After all, the building blocks of each script don't tend to vary. The key thing is to recognise the need to communicate concisely, with confidence and with concern for the writer's objectives.

- Maintain an objective tone – stick to the third person (i.e. avoid 'I' and don't address the writer as 'you'). You may refer to the writer as 'the writer', but it is best to try to stick to referring to things that happen in the script.

- Write in the present tense – the script you are reporting on is a work in progress and the present tense keeps the process alive. This is very important. Do not use the past tense in the synopsis either unless you are reporting information from the past, revealed through flashback or dialogue.

- Be specific – generalisations are not helpful to the writer and they weaken your credibility. Support all points that you make with one or two examples from the script.

- Refine your communication skills – this means thinking carefully through what you want to say and writing down your concise, conclusive comments. Do not use the page to argue out your ideas for yourself – this isn't an essay, but it is nevertheless the presentation of your considered viewpoint.

- This book provides questions to prompt your thinking in each area of the report, but be careful to ensure that your report doesn't read as a list of answers.

- Develop your own writing skills – a good report should also be a good read, elegantly written and without spelling mistakes and grammatical errors. Make sure you spell place names and characters correctly or your credibility will be diminished.

- Reference to other films can help to clarify a point but not if they are obscure – the object of the exercise is to help the writer, not to show off your own film-buffery! Do bear in mind, though, that if you read a script that is remarkably similar to a film you have seen, however obscure the film, please do mention it. This is vital information for a filmmaker that you can pass on.

- It is not your job to offer concrete or specific changes to be made to the next draft; only the writer can decide what actually must be done to improve their story. However, in exceptional circumstances it can be appropriate to offer broad suggestions; this should only ever be done in a way that encourages the writer by demonstrating enthusiasm for their story.

- Remember that witticism and sarcasm, though sometimes hard to resist, are inappropriate!

3. THE SCRIPT REPORT

The best way to organise the analytical thinking that goes into a good script report is under these headings:

- Synopsis
- Premise
- Structure
- Character
- Dialogue
- Visual grammar
- Pace
- Conclusion

The following subsections take each of these elements of screenwriting and discuss in detail how to write the most useful report on each aspect.

Before we get started properly, it is worth stating that whenever the Script Factory gathers a panel of producers or distributors to talk to new screenwriters you can absolutely guarantee that one of the very first questions will be, 'What kind of scripts are you looking for?' I suspect that, quite often, the writer who is asking is hoping to become privy to some secret industry agenda that they can go away and fulfil – films with 25-year-old female protagonists, or low-budget horror set on a Scottish island – but, without exception, the answer is always, 'We are looking for a good story.'

This answer may seem disingenuous to the new writer hoping for something more concrete, but the truth is that we all have the ability to recognise a good story. Since earliest childhood we have heard them, read them, created them, and told and retold them.

We enjoy stories for their capacity to enthral and entertain us but we also recognise the essential function of story is to help us make sense of our lives. Life as lived is a continuous series of random and unpredictable incidents over which we may only achieve a very tenuous and partial control. So, unlike the ever-evolving experience of life, stories have a very stabilising integrity. They contain a finite sequence of events that we expect to be meaningful. The stories that we consider to be good are the ones that have a sense of purpose, a reason to be told.

The most important point to remember is to be confident that you know a good story when you read one and, equally, that you know what is wrong; this book is designed to help you process your instinctive response to screenplays so that you become quick and confident in your reporting and developing.

SYNOPSIS

The most useful reports start with a brief, three-paragraph synopsis of the story of the script: a paragraph to set up the story, one to describe what then happens, and the third to reveal how it ends. This approach corresponds to the three-act structure discussed later; but, in writing a synopsis, your task is to extract the central idea of the screenplay and test whether it can be presented as a simple and consistent story, with a logical beginning, middle and end.

If the screenplay can be faithfully retold in this way it usually indicates that the foundations of a solid story are in place. The story might not be strong enough to sustain a feature film or interesting enough to warrant one, but these issues are addressed later in the report.

If it is a struggle to write a synopsis that meets basic story expectations then this is probably an indication of serious problems in the concept and construction of the narrative. The process of negotiating through the story to write the synopsis should help with the assessment that informs the later sections of the report.

Essentially, the purpose of the synopsis is to convey back to the writer the main story spine. Most writers find it very hard to reduce their own screenplays to a brief synopsis. This is because screenplays are incredibly textured documents and to ask a writer to simplify months of work into half a page of prose is daunting; it can be difficult to know where to start. A brief synopsis at the beginning of the report says: this is the main story and everything in the screenplay is going to be assessed in the light of telling *this story* well.

It is hard to write synopses, but it's a discipline that is important at the beginning of any development process because it pins down what the main story idea is and becomes the benchmark for all development.

The information in a three-paragraph synopsis roughly breaks down as follows:

1st Paragraph

- Where the story is set
- When the story is set
- Whose story it is (whether a single protagonist or a group of characters)

- The character's situation at the beginning of the film and what happens to disrupt their life and/or change their plans

2nd Paragraph

- What the character then wants or needs to do
- What stands in their way or makes it difficult
- Why it becomes more urgent

3rd Paragraph

- How the character achieves his/her goal or what happens to ultimately stop them

- What has changed about the character and/or their situation at the end of the film

The intention is always to show the story in its best light and to remember that it's a work in progress – so always write the synopsis and, indeed, the entire report in the present tense.

For example: *Juno*

Juno is 16, at high school in Minnesota
and unexpectedly pregnant by Bleeker,
after their first time, on a chair. Having
confirmed this state of affairs Juno
arranges an abortion but is unable to go
through with it and decides instead to have
the baby and give it to a childless couple
who desperately want one. Juno locates the

perfect couple, Mark and Vanessa, in the
Penny Saver small ads and decides that
these are the people that can offer the
baby a perfect family. He's cool. She's
nice, and clearly wants nothing more than
the baby.

Juno's condition raises a few eyebrows
around the school as the 'Cautionary
Whale' but her family are supportive of
her decision and all is going well - but
Juno likes hanging out with Mark and
Mark is getting too fond of Juno and the
boundaries begin to blur. Juno turns up
at the house one day to discover that her
Mark and Vanessa aren't so perfect. They
are splitting up. Distraught and eight and
a half months pregnant, Juno drives away
in crisis.

'I'm in if you're in,' Juno writes to
Vanessa and, a couple of weeks later,
as Vanessa holds her son, it may not be
perfect, but it will be okay. Juno is held
by Bleeker and assured by her dad that she
will be back in the maternity ward on her
own terms one day and, a bit wiser to the
fact that life is messy, she gets back to
being a teenager, officially in love with
Bleeker.

It is important that the reader earns their right to assess the script by demonstrating that the script has been read carefully, with serious effort being made to understand what the writer is trying to do. A well-written synopsis will assure the writer that the reader is on their side and respects what they are trying to achieve. By well written I mean that there is clearly conveyed cause and effect between the story events and not a list of events punctuated with 'this happens, then this happens, then this happens'. This style of synopsis should ensure the writer will be much more responsive to the comments and criticisms that may then be made in the body of the report.

It is important to invest emotion into each event, so, for example, instead of writing, 'John goes to see his dad who tells him that his brother was involved in a shady deal,' it's better to write, 'Desperate for information, John visits his dad who confirms his worse fears...'

The synopsis is not the time or place to offer criticism so it's inappropriate to write sentences such as, 'And then, by an unbelievable coincidence...'

Writing the synopsis isn't something a reader should labour over. The script should only need to be read once if it has been read with proper attention and the synopsis will flow better if it is written from memory. Think about it in terms of how it might be retold verbally.

That said, it is important that details such as names and places are accurate. Getting these kinds of facts and details wrong makes it easy for the writer to think that the script hasn't been read very carefully and will undermine the hard work that has gone into the report.

Summary

- Start with date and place, particularly if the story is set in the past, e.g. Chicago, 1955.

- Try to write from memory as much as possible, but check for accuracy of details (names, places).

- Use each paragraph to set up the story, describe the action and reveal how the story concludes: three paragraphs in total should be enough.

- If a whole secondary story line can be left out without creating confusion in the main storyline, leave it out in the synopsis. If a small subplot has importance, introduce it into the synopsis at the relevant time, otherwise it can be hard to refer to it later in the synopsis without extensive explanation.

- Present the script in its best light; the way to do this is convey the drama and the emotion where it is present and don't just list events in order of their happening.

- If the script is illogical or nonsensical, iron it out sufficiently in your synopsis so it can be used as a basis for the commentary. The problems will be discussed later on in the report.

- Remember the synopsis is not the place to start the commentary. Be matter of fact about the script's plot and don't try to covertly include your criticism in your use of language when summarising. Save this for later.

The synopsis should be up to a page in length.

Cameron McCracken
Managing Director, **Pathe UK**
Selected executive producer credits: *Iron Lady*, *Slumdog Millionaire*, *127 Hours*, *The Queen*

I do use script readers, and the specific skill I require is the ability to spot the strength of an idea, even if the script itself is poorly realised.

When I am reading a script the most important consideration for me to take it forward is always the strength of the concept. If the writing is good, I will pursue with the original writer. If the writing is weak, I would wish to bring on another writer better skilled in the identified area of weakness (whatever that may be e.g. humour, dialogue, action).

The only reason for passing on a project is that the concept has insufficient appeal. Some scripts are wonderfully written but it is impossible to see them ever being made because the subject matter would never find an audience (or at least not an audience commensurate with the likely budget). And sometimes, though the concept is great, after many drafts and many writers, you may simply have to put a project to one side, accepting that you haven't managed to develop a script that will satisfy an audience.

PREMISE

Having done the hard work of figuring out the story in the synopsis, the question for the premise section is: will this story make a good film? Is the idea or the concept strong enough for a feature film?

What does all drama need? The answer is conflict.

Conflict is the reason we engage with stories. As human beings we tell stories to make sense of the world, to find order in chaos, to process experience. Without conflict there is no story, simply an account of events. So whatever else can be said about the script, like the originality of the setting or the vibrancy of the characters, the one thing the success of the idea hangs on is the conflict. In every film there is something at stake that the audience can care about and identify with. This can range from something as huge as the survival of the species to something as personal as being understood.

Most screenplays play out the conflict through the experiences of one character, the protagonist. Protagonist is derived from two Greek words:

Protos – meaning 'first'
Agonistes – meaning 'a combatant, a person who acts'

From this comes the implication that a good film protagonist is one who takes action. And from that idea has developed the theory that all protagonists should have a goal. However, it is my contention that this has led to lots of confusion and lots of very bad screenwriting.

Goal implies a conscious choice, or an active desire, or a mission, and is true for films like *Billy Elliot*, where the character discovers they want or need something, and spends the rest of the film pursuing it.

However, in many screen stories characters find themselves caught up in situations that aren't consciously of their own making. They aren't proactively pursuing a desire but rather are dealing with circumstances that they didn't choose to be in. This is the case in *Juno*. Juno did not plan to be pregnant.

It is also the case that, often, what a character thinks they want is very different to what they really need. That gap between what a character is actively pursuing and what they learn along the way forms the central conflict to most rites of passage and road movie films. In *American Beauty*, Lester *wants* to shag his daughter's best friend. What he really *needs*, however, is to accept the stage of life he has arrived at and learn to be a good father to Jane. Which he does, just before he dies.

Similarly, in *Little Miss Sunshine* the Hoover family's outward goal is to get Olive to the beauty pageant so that she can have her chance to compete. But what they really *need* is to adopt Grandpa's view that it's not the winning that counts but the trying, so that when Olive stands on that stage and clearly isn't a beauty queen destined to win the crown of Little Miss Sunshine they can give her the support that every seven year old deserves and so protect her from being destroyed by failure in the way every other member of the family has been.

In more morally complex films, quite often the situation is set up so that what the character wants is actually directly at odds with what they also know that they need – a lot of good detective thrillers put the protagonist in that position, so that they are constantly getting more desperate, looking for an impossible way out of their predicament. An example of this is *Dirty Pretty Things*, where the main character Okwe wants to put a stop to the organ trafficking he uncovers in the hotel he works in illegally, whilst still needing to remain under the radar of the authorities.

When reading and reporting on scripts it can therefore be much more helpful to define the protagonist as a combatant, someone who is engaged in a struggle or fight, someone who is living out conflict. And that conflict isn't necessarily the desire to reach a defined goal. It may just be a problem.

It might not always be obvious to the character that they are engaged in a conflict – for example, victims in thrillers, or even the protagonist in a drama, might not consciously process the opposition to what they are trying to achieve, but it should be clear to the audience/reader.

In reporting on the premise in the script report there are three main tasks:

- Identify and articulate what the main conflict is
- Assess the dramatic strength of that idea
- Assess the thematic strength of that idea

How do you articulate the central idea or conflict?

The first questions to ask are: who is the protagonist? What conflict is this character facing? What do they need or want to achieve and what is standing in their way?

It can be really helpful to know that there are only three sources of conflict in the world of films:

- *Internal*, where the character's problem is made worse by aspects of their personality such as shyness, or a lack of confidence, or excessive arrogance

- *Situational/environmental*, where the character's problem is made worse by the world in which they inhabit, such as intemperate climates, the lack of anonymity in small communities, or a poltergeist in the walls

- *Interpersonal* conflicts where the character's problem is chiefly manifest through the other characters; such as a parent disallowing certain activities or a stalker that wants to steal your identity

In most film stories all three types of conflict should be evident, but in order for the story to be meaningful it needs to be informed by one clear idea and so the first task is to articulate the central story idea in terms of one main conflict. Start the premise section with a sentence or two that encapsulates the main story and expresses the conflict.

For example: *Billy Elliot*

> This is the story of 11-year-old Billy Elliot who wants to audition for the Royal Ballet School in London but he comes from a Northern mining town where boys learn boxing not ballet. Set against the backdrop of the 1980s miners' strike, this is a story about true talent emerging where it is least expected and defeating the class barriers that would hold it back.

Conflict is never original; they have all been done before. So an important element of defining the story idea or the dramatic conflict of this particular screenplay is the setting. It's the world of the story that will make it original or will give it a reason to be told again by offering new resonance to a familiar issue.

Billy Elliot has a very clear, simple conflict (which is possibly why it continues to resonate with audiences around the world to this day). It is more likely that a script will not have such a clear idea informing it and these are some of the problems that are very common:

The conflict starts late

In some scripts the main conflict doesn't become fully clear until later in the story. Often that can indicate a problem with the story design and, if this does seem to be the case, it is helpful to state that the conflict could inform the story earlier. However, be careful not to try to define the problem too early or decide that the first thing that the character seems to be pursuing is the main conflict and wilfully disregard everything that comes after.

The conflict is inconsistent

In some scripts the conflict is inconsistent, meaning that the main problem the protagonist is dealing with changes over the course of the screenplay. This usually happens when the protagonist resolves their problem and then moves on to another one. If this is the case then the premise section is the place to offer a discussion of the competing conflicts and which of them, potentially, could be developed and extended most effectively.

The wrong protagonist

It is really hard to articulate the main idea if the protagonist is not the character who is living out the most conflict. This often happens in stories with a child protagonist where the child is in fact getting to do what he or she wants, and it is the people around them that experience the conflict. (It isn't possible to tell the story of *Little Miss Sunshine* as Olive's story as it would go something like this: Olive wants her chance to compete in the Little Miss Sunshine beauty pageant, and she does.)

Not enough conflict

There are two types of instance of not enough conflict. The first is reasonably straightforward. There just isn't enough at stake to ensure that the reader/audience cares about what happens in the end. Or, quite commonly, the writer has convinced themselves that the problem is really hard to solve, because it is for their character (due to their personal hang-ups or circumstances), but, actually, in terms of recognisable human behaviour, it's really not that difficult.

Overly involved with the main character

This occurs when the story is about one main character (such as films like *Fish Tank* or *An Education*) but the writer hasn't discerned which particular aspect of the character's life the story is most interested in. In trying to tell everything about a character, the character becomes unknowable and the effect is to make the story feel crowded and not universally relevant.

Once the main conflict is articulated, the next task is to assess whether it is a strong enough idea to carry a feature film. If the main conflict isn't yet clear because of one or more of the problems outlined above, the report should assess whether the idea is strong enough once the specific problem is solved.

The most useful way to phrase the question is to ask if it offers enough dramatic potential. By which we mean: does the idea suggest that it will generate interesting events and keep the audience engaged in discovering the outcome?

Then there's the other side of the dramatic conflict...

The forces of antagonism

Dramatic potential is suggested by the depth of the conflict and
the literal number of obstacles and antagonists that the character
has to negotiate in the story. The first and most important point to
restate is that antagonism/conflict is manifest only in those three
ways – internal, situational/environmental and interpersonal, so
the antagonist or forces of antagonism are not always human. In
fact, there can be a problem with human antagonists in that they
need to be convincingly motivated and we generally don't have
archenemies in real life! However, we do have people who may
stand in the way of what we want to achieve because, somehow,
it is in conflict with what they want to do.

If the story does have a traditional antagonistic character, that
character should have compelling motivators; things like jealousy,
power, money and revenge, as well as your basic psychos. If
the story dramatises internal conflict through relationships with
people, exploring more normal situations, it is important to assess
whether those relationships demonstrate recognisable behaviour,
like parents restricting freedom, or children demanding their needs
be fulfilled, or the boss requiring commitment, etc.

If the main source of antagonism isn't another character but
the situation the protagonist finds him/herself in, then you need to
ask whether the rules of the protagonist's world, and the way they
have been set up, sufficiently restrict them from easily achieving
their goal or solving their problem? Is the internal or situational
conflict complex enough and strong enough to sustain the drama
required in a feature film? Good examples of this kind of premise
can be found in *127 Hours* and *Buried*.

Based on a true story, in *127 hours* Aron Ralston falls down a
crevice, miraculously surviving without injury, although his hand is

trapped under a boulder. There is no way of freeing it, and very little chance that anyone will find him. This is sufficiently restricting to completely engage the audience in the outcome. Similarly, *Buried* is the story of Paul Conroy, a US truck driver in Iraq, who awakes one day to find himself buried alive in a coffin, with only a cigarette lighter and a phone – enough to offer a glimmer of hope that this nightmare may end, but sufficiently restricting and horrifying to keep the audience engaged in the outcome.

In assessing the dramatic potential of the idea the main sources of antagonism should be both clear and clearly restricting. If this is not the case the 'Premise' section is the place to offer this comment and it can be appropriate to also offer suggestions about strengthening the conflict. However, be careful not to rewrite the story!

It can be helpful to consider how the conflict is layered as this is often the way that the drama is generated.

To illustrate this point clearly, consider the layers of conflict in *Billy Elliot*:

```
Billy Elliot is the story of a boy from
a northern mining community who wants to
audition for the Royal Ballet School in
London.
```

That simple description indicates that there are some very obvious potential conflicts here: he's a boy, dancing is generally considered for girls; he's working class whilst ballet is primarily the domain of the middle classes. And he lives up North and wants to go to school down South in London.

So, in the basic assessment of the idea, it is clear that there is plenty of potential conflict, but potential conflict doesn't automatically generate drama. Billy is clearly going to find it tough but it is actually the detail with which his world is set up that makes it tough enough for this to be a dramatic story.

Looking a bit more closely at the world of Billy Elliot, this is what we know: Billy comes from a working-class background, but specifically he comes from a family of miners during the miners' strike of the 1980s. This generates two key areas of conflict in the story:

- The family has no money, food is hard to pay for let alone ballet lessons and auditions.

- Billy's father and brother have a very strong sense of working-class pride, and loyalty to the cause is considered more important than personal needs and ambition. Billy's 'poofy' ballet dancing is seen as an affront to the dignity of the working man.

And in this setting, where that dignity is under threat, it's a much more emotive value and stops the antagonism towards Billy's dancing being simply inverted snobbery or chauvinist ignorance. And it's important that we do have sympathy for Billy's dad, and that would be much harder to achieve in a different setting.

These masculine values are bolstered by two further details about Billy's life: that boxing is a family tradition; and that Billy's mother is dead – without the female influence, the family is governed entirely by masculine values, and any support she may have given Billy is removed.

Finally, Billy is 11, an age at which he is still dependent on his family and therefore cannot pursue his dream without their support. If he were 15, then this would be a film about him running away to join the ballet. But, at 11, he is dependent and also at an age when he is on the cusp of developing his sexuality, so his interest in ballet triggers concern that he might be gay.

When watching the film or reading the script, all of this should just seem like character detail, none of it competing with the main conflict in the story, which is the class issue. But it is the detail that actually provides the drama: the obstacles that Billy will have to overcome in order to realise his dream.

In summary, the main conflict in this story is that Billy comes from the wrong class to be a dancer. The details of his character, situation and world enable the writer to dramatise the conflict in these ways:

Billy's **internal** conflict is his initial perception that dancing is for girls. He gets over this pretty quickly, but it is important that this argument is set up, as it will become the main objection of Billy's father, Jackie.

More importantly for Billy, his other internal conflict is his struggle with his sense of family loyalty versus his need to express himself and he's deliberately set up as a kid who is not particularly rebellious.

The **situational** conflicts in the story are the lack of money, the fact that the world of ballet is completely foreign, and that it is literally far away from home. And Billy lives in a community in which cultural pursuits are not valued.

Finally, Billy's **interpersonal** conflicts are with his father and brother, both of whom consider dancing to be for girls or 'poofs'. He therefore becomes dependent on his ballet teacher, a woman from whom he feels culturally distanced.

In other words, the writer has maximised the opportunities offered by the idea to provide the internal, situational and interpersonal conflicts that will make it as hard as possible for the character, in this case, to achieve their goal.

In reading scripts you are looking for the specific details that the writer has used which can generate the drama that the character will have to navigate to achieve their goal, solve their problem or learn their lesson.

Analysing and developing screenplays requires an ability to assess whether there are enough layers of conflict in the story and, further, that they do feed into one clear central conflict. Quite often they don't. The protagonist may have many different problems to deal with, but the obstacles and antagonism do not add up to anything consistent.

Once the dramatic premise has been considered, the next element of the premise section is to think about the thematic conflict in terms of what the story means. It seems that readers are generally happier talking about theme because it's a discipline we are used to from studying literature and it's much easier to talk generally about ideas than assess whether those ideas are played out well dramatically. Therefore, it is important to think about the dramatic premise first to stop the temptation to become immersed in the theme and meaning; to do that will fail to address the specific dramatic conflict of the story.

Thematic conflict

The story exists in order for the writer to express a view, or several views, on the world. No film can exist without a viewpoint on its subject matter. And it is in the establishment of theme that a film has resonance. It is imperative that the script report questions and analyses what a script is actually about, so that the writer becomes fully aware of the emotional, intellectual and visceral impact of their story. Themes emerge from the conflicts explored within the story, and the meaning of the film is derived from the resolution of the conflict. If the main conflict in the screenplay is unclear, it is likely that the writer's intended meaning will also be muddled. A film's meaning can be expressed as a universal 'truth' (e.g. love conquers all), personal beliefs or statements of emotional intent. These statements are often disarmingly simple, even for the most intelligent and seemingly complex films.

To analyse thematic conflict try to:

- State clearly in the report what you consider the themes, or potential themes, to be.

- Is it possible to articulate what the story is actually saying about this theme? (e.g. the theme may be 'fame', and the meaning of the story may be 'fame corrupts').

- Are the ideas in this film likely to resonate with an audience?

- Are there elements of the screenplay that create confusion by undermining the theme/meaning?

- Are events manipulated skilfully to convey the meaning, or is the message delivered heavy-handedly?

- It can be useful to offer a discussion of how the theme works in tandem with the chosen genre. For example, it would be a problem if the film set itself up as a romantic comedy but then became thematically preoccupied with something other than love.

The last point to consider is whether these themes will resonate with the film's intended audience. Effectively, the key questions are: what is at stake for the audience, either emotionally or intellectually, in this story, as suggested by the themes? How is the writer intending to engage the audience in the story?

Should the audience want the character to solve their problem or achieve their desire? And, if so, how is the specific situation of the character made universal? Whilst we may hope that Billy gets offered a place at the Royal Ballet School, the reason that it matters to audiences is because he is talented. That talent should be supported and recognised is a universal value.

To conclude the section on premise: in essence, is the idea going to take us into dramatically interesting situations and say something thematically interesting about the way people are?

Kevin Loader
Free Range Films
Selected producer credits: *Wuthering Heights, Nowhere Boy, In the Loop, The History Boys*

When I use readers I am far more interested in the summary and the judgement – including the reader's reservations – than I am in getting a detailed plot summary. If the reader thinks the script is worth reading, I'll read the script. If I want to put it into development or meet the writer, I'll read the script. There has been almost no occasion I can recall when a (sometimes far too) detailed plot summary is useful. This goes for reporting on books too!

If I'm reading a script I've commissioned then it would have to be a complete car crash for me not to give the writer another draft. If after a second go they still aren't getting to the vision we all discussed, I'll reluctantly abandon. But abandonment is such a big step – as is replacing the writer. It should be a last resort. The best thing a writer can do if they realise they are not delivering is to do another draft on their own dime – and quickly!

Sometimes I pass on a script simply because I don't want to spend four or five years of my life imagining and living in the world it creates. It's a huge commitment to make a film, and you don't get to make many; as I get older, I do increasingly feel that my choices have to be carefully made. On the other hand, I need to pay my mortgage too, so I will consider projects that I think are feasible, even if they're not necessarily something I'd have thought of, if I like the writer and feel I can do it justice. Time rarely is a factor: we all know it takes years to make a film – there's often no pressing deadline, unlike in television.

STRUCTURE

Once the idea of the story has been assessed, the report moves on to examining how well that story is being told for the screen. The structure isn't the idea of the story, then; the structure is the order in which the writer has chosen to tell it. And the choices the writer has made should be informed by, and conscious of, the way audiences receive dramatic narrative.

Many of you reading this book will be familiar with the basic three-act structure model that informs most screenwriting. Some writers vehemently reject all structural paradigms, suggesting that they restrict creativity, and others embrace them slavishly, which brings its own problems. The best advice when analysing structure is to think about how information is given to the audience; or, phrased another way, is the audience given everything that they need to know at the right time in order to be engaged by the story, understand what's going on and piece together the meaning?

That said, story structure is complex and, obviously, different genres have different requirements; it is therefore important for script readers and writers to keep studying it. Not to study the theory books but to dissect screenplays that work so as to build up a very solid understanding of how the audience's response to a story is successfully managed by a good writer.

There are key structural terms; 'inciting incidents', 'act breaks' and 'turning points', and it is crucial, as a reader, that you know both what they mean and why they matter, which is what this chapter aims to clarify.

It is important to offer feedback in a report to the writer with the assumption that they understand the structural terms. However, the task of reporting on the structure of the script is not to give an account of where the acts break and where the turning points are. That approach ensures that the report only offers a commentary on the structure rather than an assessment of how effective the current structure of the screenplay is.

The principles of screenplay structure

Fundamentally, the three-act structure works because it appeals to the way we receive stories. Film can be understood as part of an oral tradition of storytelling, because we effectively sit at the feet of the storyteller and receive the story in one continuous sitting within a limited time frame. Movies aren't designed for us to leave and come back to in the way that novels are, or even theatre is, with its literal act breaks. Because of the way we consume film stories it's imperative that the filmmaker holds our attention, and that's where the turning points come in – our interest starts to wane and so something more needs to happen to take the story in a different direction, or infuse it with greater tension so that we remain hooked to the end.

The most helpful way of thinking about structure is to be conscious of what is going on between the story on the screen and the audience. Is the audience being given the information needed to stay interested, to care about characters, to feel the tension and make sense of the story?

Act one – making it matter

The job of the first act is to make the story matter, to engage the audience in the character's predicament and to show what is at stake. It should:

Establish the tone of the film

The sooner the audience knows the kind of story they are watching, the quicker they relax and settle in for the ride. This is the reason that action films so often start with an action sequence that stands alone from the main story; its purpose is both to tell us what kind of film we are watching, and to deliver some thrills and excitement, thus buying the writer time to set up the proper story without boring us.

Scripts that deal in a particular tone, like black comedy, need to establish this quickly, and it can be really helpful for the reader to note the tone – or, more importantly, note where the tone seems to change. Black comedy, for example, often enables the audience to enjoy a story in which we treat death with irreverence, so something has to happen in the first act that signals that death is not being treated with the usual reverence; otherwise the audience won't be able to understand and enjoy the main story in the way it is intended.

Set up the world of the story

Each of the main characters should be introduced in relation to each other and to their world; the main conflict that the story is dealing in should be established and the groundwork for the themes of the film should be laid.

Contain an inciting incident that kicks the story off

The best definition of this is 'the stranger who comes into town'. It should be easy to identify what or who that stranger is, remembering that it can be as simple as a desire or an opportunity, as well as an actual person that upsets the usual order of the story-world.

And, finally, the first act ends at a turning point at which a dramatic question is raised, which should inform the action throughout the rest of the story.

It is important to remember that the 'stranger', whatever or whoever that may be, is not the beginning of the story. The beginning of the story is the decision by a character to do something (which can include not doing anything). What makes this the end of act one is the audience's understanding that this is a point of no return. It is no longer possible to carry on as things were.

For example, Lester in *American Beauty* sees Angela cheer-leading and right there and then decides he wants her. He could carry on wanting her for the rest of his life but it would be a fairly dull story. The fact that he calls Angela on the phone, and she and Jane figure out it was Lester, means this fantasy has moved into his real world. It is an irrevocable choice of behaviour and elicits reactions and responses that will need resolving.

Juno's situation at the start of the film is 'pregnant', so discovering this is not the inciting incident of this story. The inciting incident is the decision not to have the abortion, and the end of the first act is identifying Mark and Vanessa as the parents. A lot more people are about to be involved in this story. Had Juno had the abortion, life would have returned to normal with only Leah and Bleeker the wiser.

First acts should be as long as they need to be to deliver the relevant information. The basic principle is that it is about a quarter of the film's length, although different genres will need more or less.

Most early draft scripts have an overlong first act, and the probable cause is the writer setting up the world of the story in more detail than will be needed to understand the film. An audience only needs to know what is going to be relevant to the main conflict, plus an understanding of what the character is up against.

By the end of the first act, the audience should know who the story is about, why we are watching them, and they should also be beginning to care about their fate.

There are three ways that a writer can engage an audience with the character's situation and help make it matter:

Empathy

The writer can generate empathy by placing the audience in the character's shoes and allowing both the character and the audience to discover what's at stake together so that the audience becomes emotionally engaged as they do. For example, we're with Billy when he is first challenged to join the ballet class and we're with Lester when he first sees Angela.

Dramatic irony

Alternatively, a writer can engage the audience in the character's situation by using dramatic irony – which means that the audience knows more than the character does. This choice often has the effect of making an audience feel protective towards a character

– we can't turn away until we know that they know what we know they're up against.

This is routinely the case in some kinds of thrillers, in which the protagonist remains oblivious to the true nature of the threat against them until sometimes as late as the end of the second act, but the tension comes from the audience knowing what the antagonist is doing.

Intrigue

A writer can intrigue an audience by showing the character doing something that is not yet clear or understood. However, this is the most risky approach. Curiosity alone is very rarely enough to engage the audience. It is the equivalent of someone saying 'I have a secret that I'm not going to tell you'. It is hard to sustain interest in that secret for more than a moment. Curiosity coupled with a way of unnerving the audience is more likely to generate engagement. The kinds of stories that do this, and have to do this, are suspense thrillers and political thrillers. *Red Road* is a great example of this method of story telling.

In the film *Red Road*, Jackie works as a CCTV operator. Each day she watches over a small part of her world, watching and protecting the people living their lives under her gaze. The knowledge that Jackie has of the intimate and private way in which we behave when we believe we are not being watched is deeply unnerving; the cleaner dancing, the teenagers making out. This world is suitably intriguing to keep the audience engaged whilst we learn about the reappearance of a man on her monitor that Jackie thought she would never see again, and never wanted to see again. It would be harder to keep our interest in a mysterious past event without this setting.

Whichever way the writer is choosing to engage the audience in the characters and their story-world, the most important job of the first act is to end by raising a clear dramatic question. A dramatic question is the specific question that this story is going to address. For example, at the end of the first act of *American Beauty* the dramatic question is raised: will Lester get to live his fantasy and shag Angela? This informs the drama of the second act. However, as this course of action is unlikely to solve Lester's mid-life crisis, the audience raises another question, which will be discussed shortly.

The best dramatic questions are active, meaning that the answer will be in the form of a **yes** or **no** outcome. Will he get the girl? Will the murderer be caught?

One of the problems with early draft scripts is that the dramatic question is a passive one. Passive dramatic questions are those that begin with 'why'. Why did he kill himself? Why does she have to move on? Why does he have to find his real father? The problem with questions beginning with 'why' is that it is much harder to make the audience care. The writer, probably without realising, is denying the audience the opportunity to emotionally invest in an outcome. The writer is effectively asking the audience to be the passive recipient of the presentation of a character or a situation.

When preparing feedback on structure, it is important to write a decent paragraph on each act. Part of the discussion about the first act should consider whether a clear dramatic question has been raised and the report should suggest what that dramatic question seems to be. It is so important because the dramatic question should inform the development of the drama throughout the second act and be clearly answered at the climax of the film.

Be careful of being too prescriptive or critical about the dramatic question or, indeed, the lack of one. It is very rare for an early draft script to clearly present a good, clear dramatic question – however, as a reader, it should be possible to identify the general territory that the dramatic question is in, and then it can be very useful to write that in the report and indicate how it needs to be clarified. If the dramatic question is emerging as a passive one, it can be useful to pose to the writer the possibility of re-organising the material so that the question becomes active.

An example of this was a script that opened with a young man going through the increasingly horrifying routine of the things you do when you are going to kill yourself. At the end of the first act, when the character is definitely dead and his mum is about to come home, the writer raised the question: 'Why has John killed himself?' So far, in 20-odd pages of screenplay, the events have been a bit distasteful, we haven't seen anything of John that may endear him to us, nor met his mother, and it is surprisingly easy not to care why John did it. However, a shift in the dramatic question to: 'Will John's mother find out why John killed himself?' does an extraordinary thing. It changes the main character to one who is living not dead, it puts in a mission and a quest and therefore gives the story forward momentum, it creates a pathos because the character the audience is now being asked to relate to is going through something unbearable.

In terms of structure, the passive dramatic question asking 'why' generally requires a lot of backstory to come into the present of the film, which can mean an over-reliance on expositional dialogue or flashback. The active dramatic question should automatically ground the story of the film in the present. So, even though it may throw the writer of a script with a passive dramatic question into momentary chaos, it can be one of the most helpful notes in the script report.

The other thing to bear in mind is that, whilst the dramatic question should inform the drama throughout the story, and it is important that the script is consistent in exploring that question, the question can be refined as the stakes are raised.

So, for example, in *Billy Elliot* the dramatic question is first raised as: will Billy pursue ballet dancing? This later becomes: will Billy audition for the Royal Ballet School in London? It is absolutely fine for later events in the story to refine the dramatic question this way, but there must be consistency in the question. It is quite often the case that a reader needs to work backwards in order to articulate what dramatic question the first act should be posing and where it might be failing to deliver that.

It is quite useful to pause around page 30 and ask: what does the audience know about this character and the story-world so far? What question is being raised?

When there is a discrepancy between what the character wants and what the character needs, it is likely that two questions will be raised: one resulting from the character's actions and decisions and one which the audience supplies.

As previously noted, the end of the first act of *American Beauty* is when Lester calls Angela on the phone. In terms of Lester's desire, the dramatic question is raised – will he get Angela, the object of his affection? However, it is obviously not as straightforward as that. Because, from what we have seen of Lester's life so far, it is unlikely that shagging Angela is going to solve his problem. His actual problem is his mid-life crisis. The first scene of the script shown in the final cut of the film is of Jane being recorded by Ricky. She says, 'I need a father who's a role model, not some horny geekboy who's going to spray his shorts whenever I bring a girlfriend home from school.' (Filmfour Screenplay, 2000, p.1)

Lester wants Angela, but he needs to learn to love the stage of life he's arrived at and be a good father to his daughter Jane. The second dramatic question is about this.

Just to complicate things, *American Beauty* also offers a third passive dramatic question, which is: why is this man now dead? This is a very interesting device as it imbues actually quite small story events with a far greater significance because we know that there is a dramatic outcome.

Act two – making it messy

If the first act ends with a clear commitment by the character to a course of action, or a point of no return, that moment should propel the reader into the second act where the consequences of that decision begin to unfold. In *Billy Elliot*, he's decided to carry on dancing, so, for the first part of the second act, the audience watches him do that and try to keep it secret. Lester starts working out, quits his job; the Hoover family set off for California in a bright yellow VW van.

The most important point to remember is that the second act should logically develop the story. At the mid-point, the second act should contain a turning point that raises the stakes, either by making it harder for the characters to get what they want or even more important that they do. Making it messy means complicating it for both the characters and the audience. However the character first thought they were going to solve their problem or achieve their goal is no longer an option. And it is at this point that the story should restate the dramatic question. As a reader, this is what you are looking for and can offer constructive comment if the structure isn't serving the story.

A useful way of thinking about turning points is that they change the rules of the game.

The second act is generally the hardest to get right. There has to be enough happening on screen to keep the story interesting, but absolutely everything has to remain focused on the central conflict. Every sequence must offer a relevant movement towards answering the active dramatic question either by taking the character further away from solving their problem or moving them nearer to it. The assessment of the second act in a script report will mainly be about whether or not the writer has managed to do this.

The two main problems with second acts are that not enough happens, indicated by long scenes, often repeating the same beat of the story, or that too much happens around the main story, indicated by subplots taking over, or a switch in point of view to other characters.

In a script report the job is to assess whether the second act is consistent, logical and dramatic (does anything happen?), and whether it contains an appropriate mid-point that in some way shifts the power and effectively gets the audience sitting upright, re-engaged and wondering what this is going to mean for the characters. Remember to commend any sequences that work well and flag up sequences that are irrelevant to the main dramatic plot.

The second act ends at a second turning point, which signals the beginning of the build-up to the climax. This turning point further increases the stakes and raises the dramatic question again by either putting the protagonist tantalisingly close to getting what they want, with one final hurdle ahead of them to overcome, or by placing them in much more danger than they have ever been in before.

Act three – making it meaningful

The important thing to remember is that act three is a whole dramatic act, it isn't just the climax and the resolution. There should be clear dramatic events building up to the climax of the story.

The climax is generally an inevitable moment that we've been waiting for since the beginning of the film. It is a now or never moment that everything rides on. In different genres it takes different forms – in a rom-com it's usually the moment that the character realises that love is within their grasp if they risk everything and act now, generally leading to some kind of grand gesture. In thrillers it is most often a physical showdown between the protagonist and the antagonist. In dramas it is the moment that the character confronts their mother/father/lover. The climax of the film is when the dramatic question is finally answered.

The third act should also offer a resolution, which succinctly shows the consequences of the answer to that dramatic question, giving sufficient space to absorb what has happened without dragging on too long.

And, finally, the third act offers some point to telling the story by showing what the character's journey means.

In the analysis of the script's ending it is important to pick up the discussion about the meaning that is raised in the premise section. In particular, think about how the story is resolved, in terms of literally what happens to get to that point and not just the final outcome, and examine what that means. For example, does the protagonist make the choices that lead to the climax and resolution, or does another character take control?

If a clear dramatic question hasn't been raised at the outset, it becomes impossible to define these crucial moments at the end of the film. And if that's the case, that is the main point that needs to be made in the premise and structure sections of the script report.

Examples of a structural breakdown

Little Miss Sunshine based on the published script by Michael Arndt from the Newmarket Shooting Script Series, 2006

This is a story in which what the characters want and what they need are at odds, so there are two dramatic questions. The first is: will the Hoover family get Olive to the beauty pageant in time? However, as we know from the outset that Olive is unlikely to win this, the story is about the other dramatic question, which is: will the Hoover family overcome their obsession with winning before it destroys Olive too?

Olive is not the protagonist of *Little Miss Sunshine*. Olive is not living out any conflict; she is very happily getting on with her life. Richard is most often cited as the protagonist; however, given that all the characters experience change, the protagonist in this story could be seen as 'the family'.

The inciting incident of *Little Miss Sunshine* is when Olive defaults into the final of the beauty pageant. This is the opportunity that has arisen.

The end of the first act is the decision to take the whole family to California so Olive can have her chance to win the pageant. (Scene 26, p.27)

                    RICHARD
          Yes or no Olive? Are you gonna
          win?

                    OLIVE
          Yes!

                    RICHARD
          We're going to California!

The act two mid-point is the death of Grandpa. The impact of this event is that it literally slows down the journey to California as they deal with the body, and it gets rid of the only person in the family who had the right attitude to winning the beauty contest: 'A loser is someone who doesn't try.'

This is a brilliant mid-point because it impacts on both dramatic questions, taking the family further away from what they are trying to do as well as what they need to do. Really messy.

The end of the second act is when Olive gets into the contest. One question is now answered. The family has got Olive to the pageant on time, but, as we know, this is less important than the other question, which is: will it change its attitude to winning in time to protect her?

The answer is 'yes' and it is expertly demonstrated at the climax of the film where the family gets up on stage and dances. In its desire to protect Olive, and its unexpected joy at dancing and not caring what anyone at the pageant thinks, we see a new, improved and hugely changed Hoover family, very different from the one we met at the beginning.

The resolution is the moment the family is released from prison, having been arrested for disrupting the pageant (Scene 127 p.108).

> OFFICER MARTINEZ
> Okay you're out.

> RICHARD
> We're free?

> OFFICER MARTINEZ
> They're dropping the charges
> on condition that you don't
> enter your child in a beauty
> contest in the State of
> California ever again.

FRANK
(Hesitates)
I think we can live with that.

The meaning is that winning is about trying, not about winning, and when winning becomes more important than trying, it can destroy you.

The Kids Are All Right by Lisa Cholodenko and Stuart Blumberg, March 2009

The Kids Are All Right is a relationship drama about the impact of introducing Paul, the once-anonymous sperm donor who fathered Joni and Laser, into their lesbian family. The significant detail is that it starts on Joni's 18th birthday when it is only a matter of weeks before she leaves for college, with her brother Laser not far behind. The moms are Jules – a chaotic blurrer of boundaries who has spent much of the last 18 years bringing up the kids – and Nic, the protagonist, a basic control freak, for whom the value at stake in this story is the loss of control.

The inciting incident occurs when the kids contact Paul and arrange to meet him. The meeting goes well and the end of the first act is the decision to keep this momentous development secret from their moms.

The first turning point of the second act is the discovery of the secret. Paul is invited for dinner. The plan is to 'kill him with kindness and put this to bed' but Paul offers Jules a job as his garden designer. The mid-point of the second act is Jules and Paul having sex. This is the worst thing that could have happened. The end of the second act is Nic's discovery of the affair at the very moment she has decided to like Paul.

The climax is the confrontation between Nic and Paul:

```
                    NIC
        No, you hold on! Let me tell
        you something, man! This is
        not your family. This is my
        family!


    Nic slams the door in his face and walks
    back into the house.
```

As this story is about family and relationships, the resolution of *The Kids Are All Right* is Jules' speech in which she says, it's complicated but we are a family and we mustn't let anything wreck that. As with all drama stories, life goes on.

Mia Bays
MIA Films
Selected credits for marketing and distribution: *Shifty, Strawberry Fields, Tsotsi*

I use one particular reader for my own production slate – she's my right-hand woman on all company and creative matters, and so has to read everything. She works on every draft of the stuff we're making/developing. For Microwave – Film London's low-budget feature project – we do use a selection of readers, and we refresh the pool regularly, also welcoming people with real development experience to read for us, too, as we want feedback on the script, the writing, the idea and the potential to make it a micro-budget film, rather than a detailed script analysis.

In script reports, I'm looking for a clear opinion – though often I find myself going against the opinion, as I feel they've not seen the full picture! But an opinion is important, as this is an audience member responding to ideas. I don't like pedantic reporting, a reader who goes on about structure; that comes over as a snipe. The best readers are people who have some experience of filmmaking. But readers should be used as backup, not instead of the execs reading!

Tony Grisoni said a great thing at the Script Factory conference at BAFTA, which was that everyone has to be open to 'play', otherwise forget it – the script will not go anywhere and the process won't work. When I am reading a first draft and deciding whether to take it on, I look at it in a different way – it's all about the writing and then a meeting is essential. Sometimes it's about the idea in spite of the writing. But ideally it's the prowess or the promise of prowess that takes you forward.

The usual reason for passing on a project is because I just can't 'see it' or I just don't rate the writing. Although my slate might be full, if someone I trust recommends someone or something, I'll always read it and meet the writer. Most people will. Prior work is important to me. I've got to be hooked in by something.

CHARACTER

Script Factory script reports systematically order the section reporting on character after the sections on the premise and the structure of the script. This requires the reader first to consider the potential of the dramatic and thematic story and how it unfolds, before turning attention to the characters portrayed.

The main reason for this sequence is to avoid focusing solely on the characters, and even writing the whole report about them, without offering anything more substantial or helpful to the writer. Characters are very tangible elements of the story and it is possible to analyse and identify strengths and weaknesses, truths and falsehoods in their depiction. But developing characters, however strongly, in isolation to the story they inhabit will not overcome dramatic, thematic or structural problems.

It is essential to keep it in mind that problems in the premise and structure of the story need to be identified first, and that the characters must be assessed in the light of their appropriateness to the story.

Some writers create a character or a group of characters and use their knowledge of a highly developed cast to design a story (Andrea Arnold's *Fish Tank* was designed around the main character of Mia; and Mike Leigh also uses this approach.) Other writers devise a situation or a story idea and create characters to fit the drama. There is no right or wrong way to do this and both can be equally successful. The characters have to be **highly developed** and **fit the story choices** the writer has made for them.

In approaching this section of the report, set out again whose story this tells. If there are two or more key characters each of them will need to be discussed. It is rare to find a script where there are several characters whose stories demand equal attention from the audience. Much more commonly, it is only one character's problem or motivation that drives the action, impacting on other characters as it unfolds. If the script feels overcrowded with characters this needs pointing out (and this will probably back up what you have said in the premise section).

There are three main areas to consider when assessing character:

- Character Journeys
- Character Motivation
- Secondary Characters

It is important to examine the characters in the script very thoroughly; however, the precise comments may be brief and specific, which is desirable.

Character journeys

The character section of a script report examines the nature of the journey that the story is taking the character on. It is good practice to try to define the character's nature at the beginning of the story and the character's nature at the end. The distance/change/transformation/development (or not) between the two natures will enable you to start your analysis of the journey.

In film, the character's desire or need for change to happen is what drives the story. The **character's journey** means the decisions/actions that they make/take which result in some kind of meaningful change at the end of the story. There is a considerable body of 'theory' that requires characters to change their fundamental outlook or their inner nature, but this has resulted in confusion and many bad scripts.

All the books expounding these 'theories' present the idea that the best screenplays are those in which the character learns a life-changing lesson or faces the kinds of tests and challenges that alter their inner nature by the end of the story.

Consider briefly the last time you changed your attitude about something of significance? For example, about politics, religion, the death penalty, shoplifting, private schooling, or the benefit system? It is extremely difficult to effect a significant shift in attitude. If you have detected one in yourself, it may well have been precipitated by a major life-event such as a new birth, a death, marriage, or divorce. However, the prevalence of the notion that *characters change* has not been helpful, burdening screenwriters with the need to try to shoehorn life-lessons into all stories. There are many stories in which a fundamental change in a character's outlook is neither warranted nor required. And any change in a character must be brought about convincingly from the experiences that a character has been through in the course of the story.

Any film character only 'lives' within the short timespan of a film (90 minutes or so). In order to engage with *any* character's change, an audience needs first to know the character. This means being able to perceive a consistency of behaviour before any change starts to takes place. The limited time restricts the amount of meaningful change that can be shown over the course of a film. It is extremely important to approach scripts knowing how this limit applies.

Across all story types there are fundamentally three elements of the story-world that are potentially subject to change:

- The character's situation
- The character's actions
- The character's attitude

The character's situation

In every story the **character's situation** will change and that is the reason why there is a story to tell at this particular point in their lives. It may be the arrival of the Sperm-Donor Dad in *The Kids Are All Right*, or the cracks in the earth's core in *2012*. Situation, then, is the circumstances that the characters either find themselves in or actively seek to create for themselves. The situation can change in a way that isn't desired so that the film's focus is on how the character either resists the change or reverses it. In all cases, the character may or may not succeed in making or resisting the change; however, *a character in a situation and their reaction to it* is the basis of every screen story.

The character's actions

What is important to know as a reader is the difference between the **character's actions** changing and the character's attitudes changing. The character's actions are the things that the character literally has to do in response to his or her situation. And the fact that the drama of the story forces a character to behave differently to how they would on an ordinary day doesn't necessarily indicate or precipitate a change in their attitude.

The character's attitude

The **character's attitude** is the way in which the character interacts with the world, so it is shown both by the character's manner of being, e.g. aloof, happy-go-lucky, arrogant, feisty, and also by the character's attitude as shown by their belief system, their values or their worldview. A change in attitude is only warranted when the circumstances that the character experiences in a story lead that character fundamentally to re-evaluate the way they think about themselves or the world around them. Often they cannot fully complete the actions required by their situation until they have undergone that change in their attitude.

For example, Elizabeth Bennet in *Pride and Prejudice* cannot marry Darcy until she discovers that she was wrong about him and admits how prejudiced she has been. Jackie in *Red Road* will never find peace until she realises it isn't revenge that she needs, but the ability to forgive herself. On the other hand, Jackson Curtis in the film *2012* needs to draw on his resources as the earth's crust starts to crack. What is required of him to get his family to safety is the ability to drive, and he is already fully equipped with the skills and mindset to do this at the start.

Be aware of the distinction between a change in the character's actions and a change in the character's attitude. One common reason why characters 'do not work', or feel unconvincing, is that the screenwriter has not equipped them with the attributes they need to complete the action required of them. Another is that the screenwriter, to ensure that they end up in the final scenes as the character they need to be, has started them out with monumental lessons to learn that are not required in the story.

Remember also that there are stories in which the protagonist does not embark on a learning journey that alters their personality but rather follows a progression or a development, since the story is about them getting on with being who they are. Wish-fulfilment stories such as *Bend It Like Beckham* and *Billy Elliot*, or the ugly duckling stories like *My Big Fat Greek Wedding*, all feature a character who discovers they have a passion or talent. The fact that they remain dedicated to that talent or faithful to that passion enables them to overcome whatever it was about their situation that was holding them back.

Watching those films can feel like witnessing character change but it is often the case that we have witnessed not a change but a blossoming, because the world finally makes space for them to be themselves. Nothing of their inner nature has essentially changed – rather it has been set free.

Character motivation

When reading the script it is really important to note the places in it where you stop believing in a character; the scenes or sequences in which you are just not convinced that the character would say or do what they are saying or are doing.

Failing to understand a character's motivation is a very different experience from following a story that contains intrigue and/or mystery about one or more of the characters. In most situations – whether or not we have our own experience of the specific situation – there will be a range of plausible explanations that we would accept/understand, so if the character is behaving in a way that is baffling or feels unlikely, it probably indicates a problem.

The script reader's job is to examine the motivation of the characters to ensure that the writer has created consistency in action, speech and reaction that is recognisably true throughout the development of the story. There are two main problems that emerge from this examination: characters who are inconsistent and characters who are unbelievable.

Inconsistency in a character is when something in their speech or action contradicts what is already known about them, such as a character who doesn't trust anyone but stops a stranger to ask about the best restaurant in town; or the advertising executive who loathes her job and wants a new one, but knuckles down when it is under threat; or the mother who normally puts her children first, but forgets to arrange a babysitter on this particular night.

It is important to note when characters are saying or doing something that is inconsistent with their characterisation because, if the character is well thought through, these inconsistencies can readily be addressed by some additional thinking about alternatives; how else can they find out or forget in order to make the point and move the story on? (Often these flaws are hangovers from an earlier draft and usefully pointed out to the screenwriter.)

However, unbelievable characters present a much more serious problem. These are the ones where it is just not clear or plausible or viable as to why they are in their situation. Why is she still with this guy? Or why doesn't she just get another job? Or why does he decide to go on holiday to Iraq? Why does he still live with his mum?

To clarify the approach, asking **why** is natural, and all of us are engaged in story because we are interested in the particular 'why' of the situation. This is not the same as not believing in a situation in the story.

Often the new screenwriter's understanding of character comes from their observations of real people rather than studying screen characters. Real people can, of course, be deeply inconsistent and frequently baffling, whereas screen characters are entirely knowable. It is the reader's job to understand this and be able to point out the consequences of writing 'real people' rather than screen characters.

The only information that the audience needs about a character is that which will be relevant to the story. An enormous amount of thought goes into creating characters much of which will not appear in the script. The only details that should be included are those that explain why the characters are in this situation, why they can't just get out or move on, and why they do what they do.

It is very enlightening to watch films and try to write down a list of the details we know about the main character. Often there are very few. The writer's selection of details and the precision with which they are delivered distinguishes the good scripts from the rest.

Keeping an audience engaged with a character is achieved, in large part, by making the audience aware of how high the stakes are for them. The actions of the characters, and choices they make, must be difficult for them, and the audience should fully understand why they are hard, whether or not they identify with the specific situations.

As discussed in the structure section, but worth repeating here because it is so fundamental, to assist with engagement screenwriters have three points of view at their disposal:

- The audience and the character can know the same information
- The audience can have more information than the character
- The audience can have less information than the character

When the audience discovers something at the same time as the character it is incredibly powerful and films that do this the best become classics e.g. *The Sixth Sense*, *The Crying Game*, *The Usual Suspects*.

This convention can be played with, and a good example is *Shaun of the Dead*. The audience and Shaun have the same point of view in becoming aware of the ever-increasing number of zombies in London, but Shaun's failure to interpret this information correctly generates the tension and humour of the second point of view available – dramatic irony.

So using dramatic irony, where the audience knows more than the character, is an important way in which the writer is able to generate tension. The source of the tension can be fear, humour, anxiety, sympathy, pathos – all effective in getting an audience engaged. It is a very powerful tool and shows that the writer is aware of the importance of the principle *who knows what and when?* In this way the screenwriter is managing the relationships between the screen and the audience effectively.

The decision to give the characters more information than the audience is a tough one. If you are reading a script that feels boring, this may be a contributory factor. In your report, find a way to repeat the point that the audience always wants to know why a character wants or needs something, and that keeping things secret or keeping information back is not always the way to get an audience involved in a story.

Character flaws

On screen, the character's flaws are, or should be, an integral part of the story. The story itself may be about the character's flaw, or the character's flaw may be the source of the conflict that the character has to resolve (such as a crippling fear of intimacy in *Lars and the Real Girl*), or the character's flaw has some impact on how the conflict plays out.

Dwayne's colour blindness in *Little Miss Sunshine* means he can't achieve his dream of becoming a pilot, and his discovery of this propels him to expose the adults in his family for what they are, exposing divorce, suicide, bankruptcy. Here, it is a flaw in his character that drives the story.

Captain Brody in Jaws is afraid of the sea but has to overcome his fear to defeat the bigger problem of the shark killing people. In this case the audience's knowledge of the character's flaw generates dramatic irony and added tension, but, at the crucial moment, Brody overcomes it.

The way the screenwriter presents the flaws should be analysed; it is not always about showing them – it is also about how the character conceals their flaws from themselves and from others, and this can create opportunities for dramatic irony and tension. The function of flaws is that they both inhibit and enable the character's actions and, in doing so, the flaw is diminished, contributing to appropriate character change.

Secondary characters

The report must consider the secondary characters. So, first, what are secondary characters for?

- They help or hinder the protagonist.
- They provoke subplots that complicate the journey of the protagonist.
- They embody the themes of the film.
- They provide an arena within which to reveal additional significant aspects of the protagonist's character.

Are all the secondary characters contributing to the plot or the theme of the story, or revealing something significant about the protagonist? If not, their place in the story is not justified.

However, though secondary characters are primarily there to provide an environment that reveals important aspects of the protagonist, the secondary characters must also be convincing. The best way to test this is to ensure that each one has:

- Their own mini-journey
- Distinguishable characteristics
- Credible motivations

Inevitably, the screenwriter has spent much less time on the secondary characters than the principal ones, and a good report will highlight where additional work needs to be done. When considering the secondary characters it is useful to remember that **character is contradiction**. We engage because we recognise a tension between *who* they are – their circumstances and personality – and *what* they are trying to be. Obviously, the problems and desires of secondary characters will not be explored in the same detail as those of the protagonist, but they should at least be apparent.

To summarise: to make the character section of your report useful you must address different issues from the ones you have raised in the premise section. Structure this section around the following questions:

- Is the main character the one who is the consistent driving force of change, whether making a change or resisting one?

- If you are reading a script where the main character is not driving the action, the dramatic question must revolve around the search to understand the character's inactivity.

- What is the nature of the character at the beginning of the story and how has that changed by the end?

- Is the change convincing? Has it been convincingly brought about by the experiences that the character has been through?

- Is the character (and the character's journey) appropriate for this story?

- Are there too many characters vying for attention?

- Is the character's motivation believable? Do they have responses that seem appropriate for the situation and events?

- Are the stakes high enough for the character? Do we understand why it is hard for the character?

- What flaws has the main character been given? Are the flaws integral to the conflict?

- And finally, what of 'the significant others' in the story? Are they both appropriate and believable?

SCREENWRITING CRAFT SKILLS

Deciding if something is well written is very instinctive and most of us can do it. However, in a script report, the reader needs to understand both the craft and the *function* of the craft of writing a script in order to assist a writer in developing and honing good screenwriting skills. Being able to explain where the craft is not doing everything that it can is an attainable skill. Screenplays employ very specific techniques to tell their stories effectively, creating their own 'language'. Fundamentally comprising scenes, which are units of action unified by time and/or place, the dialogue, use of montage and flashbacks are all elements of screenwriting craft that are continually developing and an integral part of the experience of reading a film script. To gain fluency in the craft skills, it is worth reading a lot of good produced screenplays, because they are, simply, the best learning tool and a good read. When you begin to read scripts and write reports it is worth reading the script once for the story and then again for the way in which it is written.

There are three craft skills that the writer needs to acquire: writing dialogue, visual grammar and the pacing of the story. This section takes each of these in turn in order to help a reader understand when the language is working well, and, when it's not, to identify common problems so as to facilitate the writing of an effective script report on the craft skills.

The functions of dialogue

Keeping in mind that cinema is a visual medium and that subtext is ultimately more important than text, dialogue has five basic functions:

- To create the illusion of reality
- To advance the story
- To reveal character
- To convey information
- To set the tone

In a good script all five are continuously in play. Story, character, information and tone must all be kept in balance otherwise the illusion of reality collapses. As a principle, if one function starts to dominate – if, for example, dialogue is simply being used to convey information – the script is in trouble and a good reader needs to be able to identify instances of this.

The illusion of reality:

The primary requirement of dialogue it that it has *verisimilitude*, meaning true **and** real. The way characters speak and what they talk about must be plausible and convincing. In practice, this means that dialogue requires an ear for the rhythm, idiom and cadence of real speech, but there are, of course, many realities. Every screenplay creates its own story-world and it creates the everyday speech of that community. This may be pure invention or it may reflect recognisably 'everyday talk'. Real or invented, what matters is that the rules and conventions of the vernacular are convincing and consistent.

Advancing the story:

The commonest problem and the source of much work for script readers is noticing dialogue that fails to advance the story. The usual reasons are *repetition* and *digression*. If we can see what's happening, we don't need dialogue to explain or repeat it. Equally, when writing a scene the writer can be distracted by the *situation* and forget to develop the story. If characters are in a supermarket it doesn't mean they have to talk about the shopping list unless it advances the story.

Revealing character:

Revealing character through dialogue is, on one level, straightforward. How a character talks reflects their background, appearance, psychology and circumstances. A character may be instantly recognisable by the way they speak. The whole art of dramatic writing, however, is to get beyond the surface and reveal the truth about a character's innermost secrets and desires – their *motivation*. Dialogue should always be consistent with motivation, what a character wants/needs, but it rarely expresses it directly. The truth lies in the *subtext*. A line may express what a character feels or it may contradict it.

Conveying information:

Too much information threatens both the forward movement of a story and verisimilitude – the illusion of reality. This often happens in the *set-up* of a story when dialogue is used to convey backstory. The ensuing dialogue may have rhythm, idiom and cadence, but when characters start telling each other things they already know for the sake of the audience the story stalls and the illusion of reality is compromised.

Setting the tone:

The importance of dialogue varies with *genre*. Some demand lots, while, in others, there is less time for chat. Whatever the genre, however, dialogue has a vital role in setting the tone of the story. In a comedy we expect funny lines and feel cheated if we don't get them. Tension is enhanced through good dialogue.

Screen stories are driven by what we see. The basic principle of dramatising stories for the screen – show don't tell – means dialogue has a less demanding – if no less prominent – role than in a stage or radio play. The simplest way to reveal this is to read and imagine the script without the dialogue. Is the basic action clear? Is it possible to recognise the kind of story it is? Even with films like *Juno*, *Little Miss Sunshine* and *The Kids Are All Right*, all arguably driven to a large extent by (brilliant) dialogue, it is possible to describe the action and identify the kinds of story without the dialogue.

On the whole, though, dialogue should be concise because, in any drama, what a character thinks, feels, says and does are in conflict. The gap between dialogue and action, between what a character says and what they really think and feel, is what creates the *subtext* of a story or scene. If there is no subtext, there is nothing to discover, nothing to reveal. Good dialogue conceals as much as it reveals. What isn't talked about is as important as what is. There is a continual tension between dialogue and action. Bad dialogue has many causes but collapsing the gap between words and action is the most common.

When a reader comes to write this section of the report the questions to order thought around are these:

- Does the dialogue sound authentic for the world of story?
- Does it sound real rather than written?
- Is the dialogue badly expositional – is it telling us the story too obviously?
- Is there unnecessary dialogue? Can we see what is being said?

- Is there too much dialogue? Can scenes be written dramatically rather than spoken?
- Do different characters speak in different voices and reveal character?
- Is the dialogue assisting the story with the interplay of what is concealed rather than what is revealed?

If there are recurring problems or good examples of the dialogue not working this is a section in which page-referencing examples can be very helpful to a writer.

VISUAL GRAMMAR

This section of the script report is about the 'grammar' or the language of film, the visual techniques employed to tell the story.

The camera can go anywhere in a film and it is this freedom of movement that makes a screen story feel like a journey. We follow characters and **see** what they do rather than watch them **talk** about what they've done. The way the scenes are juxtaposed creates the language of parallel time, both in the sense that the audience understands that events are happening simultaneously, and also that the worlds of the characters are about to collide, with impact.

Writing visually

Writing and thinking visually doesn't mean *directing* the film on the page. A screenplay presents a developing action and it is customary to write how one scene connects with another (*fade in*, *cut to*, *mix to*, etc). But, within each scene, camera directions (*angle on*, *another angle*, *close up*, etc.) are inappropriate, and, if the writer includes these, it is important to make a note. Their inclusion suggests that the director won't know how to shoot the scene (whether or not the writer hopes to direct as well), or else is using it to mask the lack of real movement in the scene.

Whatever the original conception of a story, screenplays draw on a repertoire of visual storytelling techniques. **Flashbacks**, **Voiceover** and **Montage,** for example, are devices made possible by the fluency and immediacy of film. All three are essentially techniques for providing the audience with information necessary to understand the story.

Flashbacks

The argument against flashback is that it stalls the forward movement of the story and reminds us of the artifice of film. Particularly where it is used to reveal **backstory** – the history of characters or events that precede story – flashback can feel like bad exposition. However, there are many good examples of effective flashback that allow the writer to heighten a moment or to illuminate an action or character. For example, *The Sixth Sense* revisits all the scenes in which we understood Dr Malcolm Crowe to be alive and enables us to reinterpret them with the new information that he is dead. *The Usual Suspects* flashes back at the end to enable us to see the truth.

As a rule, if flashbacks represent a character's *subjective* understanding of the past – speculation about a crime, a puzzling memory – they don't disrupt forward movement because the story is about the character's developing understanding of the past. In such cases, flashbacks are motivated by the character's need to discover the truth. *Objective* flashbacks need much more care. When assessing these kinds of flashbacks in a script, you need to ask yourself whether the audience needs to see a past event in order to fully understand the present. On the whole, flashbacks work if they offer insight and allow us to reinterpret information that we already have, rather than just delivering information. If the script you are reporting on has flashbacks, the question must always be: what is their purpose? Are they adding insight? Or can the information be incorporated into the present of the film?

Voiceover

Voiceover narration is of two basic kinds: interior and exterior. **Interior narration** allows us to hear the private thoughts of a character as they reflect on the events of the story. The intimacy encourages the audience to engage with the character's thoughts and feelings. This is particularly useful where a character is difficult to identify with. For a good example of this, read or watch Barbara's voiceover in *Notes on a Scandal*.

A problem arises when the voiceover is failing to add insight, pathos, humour or tension, and is either telling us what we can see, or telling us what we should be able to see with a bit more thought on the possibilities of dramatisation.

Exterior narration, the objective voice of the storyteller, is rare in contemporary cinema.

Montage

Montage is compressed drama: a series of images that tell the audience an **important** part of the story. A montage of someone getting up, brushing teeth, shaving, eating an egg and closing the front door is unlikely to be a crucial part of the narrative. The audience does not need to see the detail to understand a character has got up and left the house. Good montage is making use of the economy of screen time by appealing to the ability of the audience to move the story along. There are two points to consider. The first is that montage is expensive. Hauling a film crew to many locations for a second or two of screen time in each has got to justify its place in the story to justify the budget. Secondly, when it is done well and is integral to the story it can be brilliant, so there is a fine judgement about the effectiveness of any montage sequence that a reader must make. Stories that take place over time and require character change may rely on montage to speed up the story. Romantic comedies often use montage effectively.

Special effects

Special effects are usually employed in specific genres, most obviously science fiction. Advancing technology means that almost anything can be achieved on screen, so, rather than complicate this, if you are reading a script in which special effects are required, the question you are asking is whether the world of the story is believable and credible, so that the effects feel integral to the story rather then clever techniques.

The visual grammar is the way in which we see the action: the action is what happens and the grammar is the way in which we see it.

In summary here, this section of the script report asks – does the writer show an understanding of the grammar of visual storytelling? The reader should comment on the ways in which the writer tells the story 'cinematically' i.e. consider the techniques that are uniquely available to the screenwriter and how they are deployed in the script being read.

When thinking about this section it may help to order your thought as follows:

- Is there an understanding of the craft of visual language in the script? What is the use of visual grammar contributing to the script?

- If the script contains few or none of these techniques, could it be improved by their use?

- Is the movement between scenes effectively creating a sense of parallel action which builds anticipation and adds to the tension or comedy?

- Does the use of visual grammar play a useful part in creating dramatic irony?

- Is this a story that could use montage effectively? Is there opportunity to compress a long sequence of scenes through montage? Or, is montage used inappropriately?

- If voiceover is used in the script assess how effective it is in creating empathy with the character or adding tension to the story.

- If there is use of flashback/flashforward is it expositional or does it really enhance the story?

PACE

This section of the script report deals with the technical skill demonstrated by the writer in modulating the tempo and mood within the script, not with the overall structure of the story. Remember that the script is a blueprint for a work that is destined (hopefully) for the screen and, while a script that is a real 'page-turner' may translate into a well-paced film, many movies that feature long action sequences can be difficult to read.

Pace is about the movement in the film and to some extent governs *how* the audience becomes emotionally involved in a story on screen. Modulating the tempo is a very sophisticated technique and, unlike music, where there are many tempos, there are three in screenplays which are all extreme. One is **real time**, one is **slow motion** and the other is **compressed time**.

Compressed time

On the whole, the audience can do much of the work in a film: we don't need to see someone turn a handle, come into the room, sit down and start talking. Instead, the writer can cut straight to the conversation and we understand that all action before the conversation has happened offscreen. A good reader looks at the structure of the scenes to see whether they are as economical as possible; are they allowing room for the audience to bring its own inferences and assumptions to the table?

Slow motion

This tempo is more usually the choice of the director, but can be used by the writer to emphasise an action in the script; slowing down what happens enables more significant impact, such as a gunshot. If slow motion is used in a script, is its function to create impact, so the audience does not miss the moment?

Real time

This is watching action over the time frame that it actually happens and its function in scripts is to emotionally engage the audience in the situation. Using real time enables the audience to more clearly experience the pain, the dilemma or the pleasure of a character and, in so doing, the audience comes to care more.

When writing this section of the report it can be helpful to organise the response through these questions:

- Is this script a page-turner or is it slow and laborious to read? Does it demonstrate an ability to vary the tempo?
- Do key scenes start and end at the optimum moment?
- Do the scenes vary in length and mood so as to emotionally engage and affect the audience?
- Do sequences build to create tension or humour?
- Is real time used to engage an audience?

Martha Coleman
Head of Development, **Screen Australia**

When I am reading a script, the most important consideration to take it forward to another draft is whether or not the underlying premise is strong enough to carry a 90-minute cinematic film, no matter what kind of story it is. And whether there is potential for engaging characters to keep the story moving.

When passing on a project it's always about the project itself, never about the time. Some projects take years to get right. Often it's because we feel the team have taken it as far as they can without reaching its full potential, either because the craft is just not good enough or the vision – what they want to say – is, in our opinion, not strong enough. Often it's because we have come to the realisation that the premise does not, after all, have the weight to carry a 90-minute film.

Screen Australia use a small pool of script readers, all of whom have a good grasp of screen craft in all genres. It's important to us that the readers are not arrogant and they are able to critique a script with a desire to understand what the writer's intention is and with a respectful approach.

I have taken on projects that need a lot of work and managed to negotiate the changes successfully with the writer. It's always about understanding what the writer's intention is, helping to identify and prioritise the blocks that are getting in the way of what s/he is trying to say and helping to guide the writer to remain focussed on what s/he is trying to say in every scene. The best strategy is clear, constructive communication.

Another important deliberation when we are considering a project is whether the project is achievable for a budget commensurate to its likely audience. Similarly, we may decide to pass or discontinue developing if we feel the filmmakers have an unrealistic expectation of budget level for their film or they are unwilling to work on reducing the budget to an appropriate level for the film they are making.

FEASIBILITY OR CONCLUSION

This is the last section of the report and, if it is intended for the writer, this is where the main points of the report should be briefly summarised and some comment made on its feasibility in terms of 'market'. It is not the script reader's job to guess at the budget or the difficulties associated with locations or special effects, and it is inappropriate to expect readers to do this. However, the consideration that the reader has given the script does mean they are best placed to raise questions for the writer to think about in terms of development required and market potential. The main job of the conclusion is to be clear about the priorities for the next draft – the most important issues to address if it is to find an audience.

And that concludes the script report.

4. A SAMPLE SCRIPT REPORT

Broken Heart Boot Camp by Alexandra Wilds
(Second Draft)

Synopsis

The story is set in the present day in London and Derbyshire.

30-year-old Elle has just been dumped by her boyfriend Jonathan. He claims he needs to devote his efforts to making a success of his restaurant, and she has bought it, believing it's only a matter of time before he'll be back with her. However, one disastrous and humiliating night at the restaurant makes it crystal clear that the relationship is over. Witnessing her public heartbreak are diners Tom and Hope Brightside, who run Broken Heart Boot Camp, a weekend of exercises for body and soul guaranteed to mend your heart and set you on the path to finding your true love. Hope presses her business card into Elle's hand saying the best way to get him back is actually to get over him. That night Elle signs up.

Also at the boot camp that weekend is Will, an undercover journalist, there under protest to write an exposing article for his godmother's magazine. If he doesn't deliver, he can kiss his job goodbye.

Will is immediately taken with Elle but she has her mind firmly fixed on getting Jonathan back and has no time to listen to her own heart, which is - definitely - being tugged towards Will. Stuck in the middle of nowhere on a bonding exercise, Elle finally falls for Will but, with typical bad timing, the experiences at the camp have reminded Will that love is too risky to try again.

Will's cover is blown just as the camp is swamped with press and it is assumed that he has betrayed the vow of secrecy that everyone has signed up to. However, although this was his original intention, it wasn't actually him. Elle leaves the camp with her heart mended and determined to get over men and get on with life. Will does write his article, but, rather than the exposé he was supposed to submit, it is a heartfelt piece about his

own disastrous love life and his instinct
to sabotage the next relationship, just in
case. He is clearly talking about Elle. Now
that Will has been vindicated - he wasn't the
one who exposed the camp - boot camp friends
engineer to get Will and Elle in the same
place. There is a bit of panic and flurry at
the end as Jonathan shows up, but eventually
Elle and Will kiss. It is the beginning of a
new chapter of love.

The Premise

Broken Heart Boot Camp sits squarely in the
territory of classic romantic comedy. Elle is
the protagonist who wants to get her boyfriend
back, but it is pretty clear that he has no
such intention. Elle's main conflict is her
refusal to see the truth of the situation, and
her decision to go to the Broken Heart Boot
Camp is motivated purely by her desire to get
Jonathan back.

The problem with this set up is that the
audience is required to invest in Elle coming
to realise that she is being a fool, and
whilst the situation can certainly elicit our
sympathy it is possibly unlikely to engage our
empathy. This is compounded by the very late
introduction of the real love interest, Will,
and it may be worth considering how to bring

Will into the story earlier. Once the audience recognises that Will can mend her broken heart if only she lets him, this creates a solid premise for a romantic comedy: in order to move on in love, we need to get over the last one.

The dramatic potential of the idea is currently weakened by the way the conflict is set up. Jonathan, who is the major obstacle to what Elle wants, is introduced briefly in the opening scenes and not seen again until the closing scenes. This renders Elle's conflict almost entirely internal for the bulk of the story and the effect is to narrow the possibility for both comedy and drama; Elle is 'fighting' with herself and, whilst this is a key aspect of the genre, it needs to be made both external and humorous through careful plotting of events. The boot camp - which is a unique and fantastic setting for a romantic comedy - can offer a range of situations that enable Elle to realise that her heart is mending whilst at the same time bringing her and Will into a relationship that can elicit the audience's investment.

In terms of the stake, it isn't clear that Will is 'the one' for Elle until the revelation in his article and the climactic scenes. Holding this back helps to ensure the ending is powerful; however, the opportunity to observe that they would, and could, be perfect for each other during their time at boot camp would allow the audience to invest in this ending more effectively.

The subplot of the boot camp in financial difficulty, whilst providing additional drama, detracts from the meaning of the story. Will's article at the end of the story generates lots of customers for the boot camp, so it confuses the point of the story and leaves us wondering if saving the business, rather than mending hearts, is the priority? Tom and Hope seeking out clients does certainly add humour but these scenes can probably be incorporated without the financial crisis.

As a romantic comedy, this script makes some astute observations about the nature of love, and specifically how a broken heart doesn't destroy you. This is likely to resonate with contemporary audiences. The setting of the boot camp also contributes to the contemporary feel; creating a world where ambitions are revealed and feelings are shared as a normal and natural part of the day is a phenomenally useful device.

Structure

Broken Heart Boot Camp sets up the tone of a romantic comedy with skill and economy in the opening scenes; Elle is introduced in a very recognisable exchange between 'the broken hearted and her best friend', who is imploring her not to make an idiot of herself, which, of course, she does. The world of the story is clear and an effectively benign world for the genre. However, the key structural beats need considering. In order to make this about the new relationship rather than the old, bad one, all the turning points should relate to Elle and Will.

Because of the problem in the set-up of the story and characters, the inciting incident seems to be the rejection of Elle by Jonathan, and the end of the first act is the arrival at boot camp. But she has arrived to mend her heart in order to get Jonathan back, so it is literally a long time before she notices Will. If the story is reconsidered to make meeting Will the inciting incident of the story and the reason, perhaps, that she must get over Jonathan, these structural issues will by default be reordered. It would also help generate a dramatic question that would enable the audience to invest in the outcome. At the moment, it is somewhere in the territory of: will Elle mend her broken heart and get Jonathan back? And it needs to be more like: will Elle realise that true love is within her grasp if she can mend her broken heart?

The second act follows Elle's commitment to the boot camp regime, and, whilst there are imaginative exercises for the campers, there are a number of 'emotionally' repetitive scenes in which Elle restates her determination to get back with Jonathan. This is affecting the pace and slowing it down, as the audience is ahead of the character, knowing this is not the right course of action. The mid-point seems to be Elle's realisation that Will could be the one, just as he decides to give up on love. Whilst this is a 'classic' rom-com moment, there has not been enough contact and drama between these characters to make it meaningful and give it the impact that will drive the story to its climax. With a clearer set-up of the real interest in this story, the dramatic question and the second act will be easier to develop.

Despite the problems in the set-up and the developing action of the second act, this script has a very classic climax and resolution, with the lovers being brought back together by their new best friends, misunderstandings banished, and an ending on a kiss. The third act has confidence and lots of pace.

Characters

Elle and Will are the main characters.

Elle starts out as a broken-hearted woman, investing all her hope into mending a bad relationship. By the end of the story she is happily kissing Will, with new friends, a good job and a mended heart. The actions and decisions that she has taken - to submit to boot camp - have been justly rewarded.

Elle is both driving and resisting the change in her situation; she wants things to go back to what they were, which makes her a strangely passive character. It is difficult for the audience to invest in what she wants and the current set-up of the story doesn't yet enable investment in what she needs, because that - or Will - isn't in the story enough, or appropriately.

It is fine to have a protagonist who wants and needs different things in romantic comedies. At the moment, Elle's explicit desire to get Jonathan back, though not unbelievable in terms of human behaviour, makes her a bit of a fool and her characterisation is teetering dangerously close to 'pathetic' because it is not clear why Jonathan is so desired. The decision to go to boot camp is born of desperation and it may be worth considering the other possible and plausible motivators that would counter her passivity, and invest it with more comedy. This aspect of her character is reflected at boot camp where Elle takes a very obedient position in the boot camp world, impacting on both the potential for comedy and for drama.

Will is a car-wreck kind of guy. He has a failed marriage, he's on the edge of his career and about to fall off, and unwilling to invest in love again. He, too, is appropriate for the genre, and his mission to expose the camp contributes nicely to the plot. His change of heart is revealed in his article, which is a good device for full character revelation. However, it is a little clichéd that Will is sent to do an exposé on the boot camp as his last-chance-as-a-journalist scenario. It could be nicely complicated, and perhaps feel more truthful, if he were to seek out the camp and propose the article, going undercover for journalistic purposes but having a personal motivation for being there, too.

The two secondary characters at the boot camp are nicely balanced to add to the themes and the humour, each with a successful mini-journey. Alpha's trust in her childhood sweetheart is vindicated and they get married; Alice replaces the cardboard cut-out with a real Goth and learns that a boyfriend that talks to you isn't necessarily a bad thing. Hope and Tom are the characters that could

benefit from some more thought. The main beat
in their relationship is panic over business
and money, which feels slightly at odds with
their philosophy.

Dialogue

There is a lot of dialogue in the script,
which can be appropriate for the genre,
and much of it is funny and well observed.
However, the story is too reliant on dialogue
as its main driver and, as a result, it is
often repetitive. (Elle's cry that she wants
everything to be as it was before is stated
several times.) A more considered developing
action-line at the boot camp would help to
address this. At the moment, many exchanges
lack any subtext and the ones required to
deliver information could be much more precise.

Visual Grammar

This is a story with limited use of cinematic
techniques but it still has a strong visual
sense. This is helped by the climactic set
piece, which is wonderfully visual, and the
whole pink-tracksuit-plus-muddy-assault-course
world of the boot camp. To effectively balance
the stories of the protagonists at the start,
some consideration of the use of parallel time
is required. Elle and Will need equal screen

time; understanding who Will is, and what
his situation is at the start of the story,
intercut with Elle's opening scenes, would
help ensure the audience is invested in the
right outcome - that they should be together.

Pace

This is a story that mostly takes place over
48 hours with a break before the climax and
resolution. It should be a pacy good read once
the key issues of the premise and structure
have been addressed. At the moment, the pace
slackens in the middle because of the lack
of events and the internal nature of the
main conflict, and many of the scenes are too
long - especially those with exchanges of
dialogue. There are 81 scenes in a 91-page
script, clearly indicating that many are too
long - the optimum number of scenes to aim
for is somewhere around 130. Once the overall
structure is solid there should be room to
vary the pace so we can career through most of
the story but spend real time with both Elle
and Will as a way of emotionally investing in
their 'togetherness'.

Feasibility

Romantic comedy is an eternally popular
genre and *Broken Heart Boot Camp* offers a

contemporary setting to an age-old story that
will have the power to resonate with wide
audiences with some development.

The priority for the next draft is to think
about how to enable the audience to fully
invest in the idea of Will and Elle being
together, rather than with their past loves.
This will help to keep the main conflict and
the structural beats about the relationship,
where they should be, and this in turn will
help clarify the dramatic question and address
the issues of the pacing.

5. WRITING AND ASSESSING TREATMENTS

There is no agreed film-industry definition or standard for treatments. They are often referred to, and regularly required, as if it can be assumed that we all have a complete and clear understanding of what to do. This chapter will analyse the subject and will offer some commonsense guidance to readers who may often be asked to assess treatments, as well as to script developers and producers who may find themselves writing one, not to mention screenwriters.

THE PURPOSE OF TREATMENTS: WHAT ARE THEY FOR?

- The most common purpose of the treatment is to set out the writer's or producer's proposal for adapting for the screen a story from another source. In this case the idea for the story already exists as a book, a play or other form, and the purpose of the treatment is to express the story for the screen.

- Treatments are also useful for original film ideas: to provide the writer with a brief, working document; to help ensure the premise and structure are sound in advance of writing the first draft; and also to obtain feedback from a reader at this stage.

- During the script development process (see the next chapter), when significant changes to the premise or structure are being tested, it is often advisable to write a treatment rather than another draft.

- A treatment may also be a proposition document for an original idea, intended for producers or funding bodies.

- Treatments are also regularly required for applications to project-focused training courses and for development funding. When the treatment is a requirement, it is likely that guidelines will define what should be incorporated into the treatment, including how long the document should be.

However, with at least five different functions and different users to address, the treatment is defined for our purposes here as the prose version of the story of the film, and it should be between three and ten pages in length.

Treatments have acquired a reputation for being hard to write and not usually well written. Consequently, there are many producers and developers who don't like to read treatments and who prefer to read a full script. Within 20 minutes of reading 30 pages of a script, an experienced producer can decide with confidence whether or not there is a good story, and whether or not the writer has skill and talent. A treatment can make its reader hesitate, asking: is it possible that there is a really good idea lurking in this largely nonsensical text? Or the reader perceives that the idea in the treatment is great, but can the writer craft a great screenplay?

Nevertheless, treatments are frequently requested and, whatever the intention, we can say that their main function is to get to the heart of the story. Often, however, writers do not know that this is what is expected of a treatment. One problem in particular is the notion that it is a sales document for the script, leading the writer to employ selling techniques in the treatment, e.g. stressing the 'unique selling points', the potential cast, the target demographic. Never forget that the strength of a script is measured by the story it tells. That, of course, means the whole story: the beginning, the middle and the end. A treatment should not simply state the source of inspiration or a single idea. These have to be followed through to demonstrate a convincing and meaningful proposal.

It is very important that the treatment encapsulates the story rather than talking about it like a film review (e.g. 'This film is a fast-paced contemporary reworking of a classic Hollywood story...'). This approach will not engage the reader in the situation and the characters but instead distance the reader from the story.

Presenting the treatment as a teaser sets up the story and then either doesn't state the ending, or else lists the various possible outcomes. Without knowing the resolution to a story the reader may not be able to divine its meaning and is denied the information to assess the idea adequately.

Treatments frequently give too much detail, including too many random characters and too many names. In a short document it is more helpful to identify the significant secondary characters with their names and definers – brother, teacher, neighbour, vicar, etc – when they are first introduced in the story (e.g. 'John the vicar...'), and then, later, when they appear again for their significant action, by their definer only. ('The vicar rings the doorbell', rather than 'John rings the doorbell', avoids the need for the reader to turn back to check who John is.)

Occasionally, it may not be clear from a treatment whose story is being told or which point of view the reader is being asked to adopt. This is usually the case when the writer has to lay out backstory at the beginning, or if the treatment starts with information about a character who is either secondary or not the main character. If it isn't immediately clear whose story it is, better just to state it at the start.

Because treatments are so often seen as a necessary evil, they are not given the attentive care that writers give to their scripts, and the storytelling technique is not sustained throughout the document. Like a newspaper article where the first paragraph is really gripping but the details that follow seem rather dull, treatments that simply list the literal beats of the story but lack a strong narrative flow are hard to engage with. Treatments should not be formal but, like all good writing, they should be written with spirit, imagination and expression.

GOOD TREATMENTS

A good treatment has to be well written with a sure narrative flow. The writing should be strongly visual, enabling the reader to 'see' the characters and the story-world and to hold them in their imagination as they read.

Writing a treatment: where on earth to start?

What the reader wants to know as quickly as possible is what sort of film this is. They want to be able to recognise the broad shape of the story and there are several ways a writer can help them do this. One of the key things in being able to recognise something quickly is that you can see it all. So it may be worth considering a thumbnail sketch of the whole film at the start of the treatment and then gradually build up to a bigger, more detailed picture, before zooming in for a close-up on some elements.

Obviously, no one can write a good treatment until the premise of the film is completely clear and, by the same principle, it will help the reader if the treatment offers them one or two sentences at or near the start of the document that summarise the essence of the story: who is it about? What is their main problem? Do they solve it?

Or it may be helpful to pose a question to the reader. A 'what if...?' scenario that indicates the main dramatic situation that the story will explore. It is not necessarily important to answer the 'what if...?' at the outset, but to present an intriguing enough situation that the reader has a reason to carry on.

Most important is to ensure that you strike the right tone for the story to be told and the genre it is in.

Striking the right tone

The tone of the film is intimately connected to its genre: it is the way in which the depiction of the story-world supports the underlying meaning of the story, and the worldview of the writer. Hence, romantic comedies feel light and sunny (Is it raining? I hadn't noticed...!). A dog flattened by a car in a broad comedy may be a tragedy for the owner but is a joke for the audience, whereas a dog hit by a car in a drama (in which the tone is very 'real world') is a shocking moment for both the characters and the audience.

The audience for the treatment is the reader and one of the considerations should be about the ways to control how they feel as they read. The choice of vocabulary is an important way in which you reflect the story-world. So 'The lads pile in the motor and burn rubber up the Old Kent Road' paints a very different picture from 'The men get into the car and set off at great speed down the Old Kent Road'.

If style and tone feel problematic it is likely that the problem is in the story, probably because it is trying to do too much in this respect. In other words it is a mix of genres. It is hard, for example, for a story to be both a rite of passage and a thriller; the tone, the pace, the character journey, the world and the resolution of these kinds of stories are all different.

Remember that if the treatment is for a comedy film it should be funny!

In trying to capture the essence of a story in a sentence or two, it can be helpful to work through it logically. Who is this story about, what is their problem or situation, and what happens at the end?

For example:

```
Romeo falls in love with Juliet, daughter
of his father's sworn enemy and, in the
struggle to overcome the opposition to
their marriage, both of them die. Their
untimely deaths bring about the end of the
feud between the two families.
```

However to express it like this tells the reader the tone:

```
When Romeo crashes a rival gang party and
finds himself face to face with Juliet they
```

```
both know in an instant that their lives
have changed for ever. What they cannot know
is how short their lives have just become.
Tragic accidents and misunderstandings leave
both of them dead, but at least the bloody
gang war is finally over.
```

The reader knows (even if they had never come across Will Shakespeare!) that this film is a tragic love story in an urban gang setting. In this instance there is no need to spell out that the genre of the film is a tragic love story or flag up its themes and/ or controlling idea because all of this is obvious from these few sentences.

However, there may be other sorts of stories in which the reader will need more of an obvious steer.

The world of the story

If the setting of the story is likely to be unfamiliar to the reader, for reasons such as it is in the past or the future, or is in a country or region that is not well known, or is set within a community that has its own particular customs, it is important to ensure that the rules of that world are made clear to the reader early on.

If it isn't indicated otherwise a reader will assume that your story is set in the present day and in the city and country in which they are reading it and this often leads to subsequent confusion that can prejudice their response to the idea.

It can be effective to state a fact because, if it's an intriguing one, it is also likely to serve as a hook.

Mr & Mrs Smith could have effectively started with a statement that says:

Professional assassins all lead a double life. To their friends and neighbours they are happily married, conventional, law-abiding members of neighbourhood watch, but it's just a cover. Even their husbands and wives don't know that, whilst everyone else is doing the school run or the daily office grind, they are bumping off politicians and annihilating business men. Jane and John Smith (not their real names) are New York's top-secret assassins. So secret that neither has a clue what the other really does for a living...

Screenplay structure

It is essential that the treatment reveal a good understanding of screenplay structure and the best way to convey this is to:

- Establish the normal world of the main character
- Describe what happens to kick start this particular story
- Articulate the active, dramatic question that runs through the film
- Indicate the layers of conflict that will keep things developing through the middle section of the film
- Describe the climax, i.e. the final confrontation with the main source of opposition/antagonism – and tells us which way it goes
- Resolve any outstanding important story threads

Remember to write in a way that constantly reminds the reader what kind of a film this is, not just with the vocabulary you choose but by varying the lengths of the sentences to reflect the pace of the action and by drawing the reader's attention to visual imagery if this conveys important layers of meaning in the story.

Dialogue

If the project is a soft-concept drama or a sophisticated comedy it is likely that dialogue will be doing more work than it would in many of the other genres, so the treatment should probably be well sprinkled with exchanges that mark key turning points or big laughs.

Writing visually

It can be tempting in writing the prose version of the film idea to drift into novelising the story: this means writing too much description, supplying more character backstory than necessary and telling the reader the stuff that is going on inside the character's head. Writing in the present tense should help keep it focused on the fact that this is a film, and remember that, in films, the vast majority of key moments are marked by what the characters DO and not what they THINK. Constantly check that the writing is telling the reader what is happening in a way that conveys the action from what they are seeing. In a story in which the plot turns on subtle changes in a character, make sure that it is clear how these changes will be signalled to the audience.

It can be worth considering whether to open the treatment by describing the action of the first scene rather than telling the reader about the main character. Characters come with backstory and the temptation to drift into this in detail can make the reader panic – how will I know all this from what I see on the screen?

Read back each paragraph to ask whether there are any concrete images conveyed; can the reader see someone doing something or is it vague? This doesn't mean that everything that happens in every scene needs to be described in detail, but the writer should choose pivotal moments and make sure that the treatment conveys how the film plans to TREAT that revelation, plot development, character reveal in a dramatically interesting way.

The setting of the film in general, and key scenes in particular, is obviously an important element of what makes the story cinematic, but hone the skill of painting the scene with the minimum number of brush strokes. If a scene is happening on a beach in the north of England in winter, how much more information does the reader really need in order to visualise it?

Introducing and describing characters

Keep the number of characters featured in the treatment to the minimum necessary to convey the essential elements of the film. It's important to name the key characters but it is even more important to introduce them with the significant detail that pins down the kind of person they are. An indication of age is always useful (unless it is obvious from the context) but race and physical attributes should only be highlighted if they are significant in terms of the character's role and behaviour in this story. Far more useful to the reader trying to hold the cast in their head as they read is a pithy phrase that evokes the character's general demeanour or attitude: Greg is a looker and, boy, does he know it; Juliet is a solemn 10-year-old with eyes that have seen worse things than you can possibly imagine, etc.

It is also important to avoid giving too much precise physical detail about characters so that the reader can fill in the detail that works for them. If, for example, it's important to your story that a character is fantastic looking and you describe blue eyes, blonde hair, etc, but the reader doesn't go for that physical type, you are giving them a way out of engaging with your character and therefore your story. Far better to say something like: Jane walks into the restaurant and heads turn – every woman in the place wants to be her and every man just wants her.

These principles also apply to establishing what is significant in the character's emotional or professional life. Of course, the treatment could just state that they are in an unhappy marriage, or hate their job, but it's far better, both in terms of evoking the film and engaging the reader's active investment in the story, if the treatment describes briefly the scene that conveys this information:

```
John is in his pyjamas standing outside
the bathroom door. He raises his hand to
knock but thinks better of it. The door
opens. Suzie walks past him without a word,
pulling her robe tightly around her.
```

Point of view

It is important to ensure that the POV is clear. In a single-protagonist film this will mean writing the treatment from the main character's understanding of the story. It is not unheard of for treatments to be written in the first-person voice of one of the characters, but clearly this is only appropriate if it is an accurate reflection of the film, and if that character has a distinctive voice. This kind of limitation on the writing can be creatively liberating for the writer but it can also compromise what the treatment can actually achieve for the reader. It is likely to work best in relation to films in which the whole script is written solely from the main character's POV and less well in relation to films that depart from that to an objective POV. It is quite possible to strike a happy medium by alternating the 'voice' of the treatment between that of the character and an objective voice. If this approach is used it is probably a good idea to employ a simple, obvious and consistent layout convention to distinguish between the two.

What to do with a multi-strand story?

Multi-strand stories are those that have several discrete story lines each with their own beginning, middle and end. The disparate stories may be connected by a key event, or by a place, or through a theme, and ideally all three, to generate a cohesive film, but each strand is also complete within itself. (Examples of multi-strand films are *Crash*, *Magnolia*, *Love Actually*). A film in which a single story is followed may still use different points of view to show different events, as is the case in *American Beauty*, but, ultimately, if one story is being told (in this case Lester's mid-life crisis) it is not a multi-strand.

When preparing a treatment for a multi-strand story, a good question to ask is what links the individual stories and then to flag that up strongly at the beginning of the treatment. It may be that they are all set in the same location but there is also likely to be an event or theme that links the characters. If it is an event – such as a car crash and the ramifications of that on several lives – then, wherever that happens in the film script, it is a good idea to begin the prose version with that event.

If the characters are linked thematically (grief, trust, love), it is likely that each character will bring a different point of view to the theme to give the story a wholeness and sense of completeness. Ensure that the way in which each character is introduced, and the way their actions are portrayed, clearly distinguishes each character's position in relation to the central theme.

Think very carefully about whether to intercut between all the stories in the treatment in the way that the script does. Obviously, the more strands there are, the harder this will be for the reader to follow, and it may be better to give one small indication of the way the film will move between characters early on in the document but then simply to summarise each character's story.

Acknowledge the source

If the film is an adaptation of a book (or anything else), or is based on a true-life event, then be sure to flag this up at the start. The industry is notoriously conservative when it comes to totally original material so make good use of the advantage that an existing source endows on a project. However, be even more sure that all the underlying rights have been secured before approaching the industry with a treatment or script.

Finally – make it reader-friendly

The people who will be reading the treatment spend most of their time reading scripts. Scripts are documents with lots of space on the page and this has a psychological effect on the reader that is very different from reading blocks of prose. So aim for a layout that is elegant and well spaced, with wide margins and a 12-point font. Avoid colours and quirky fonts. Keep the paragraphs short and, where appropriate, break up chunks of prose with short extracts of dialogue. The convention is to write treatments in the present tense in order to keep the reader involved as the action develops.

As with all aspects of screenwriting, there is no magic formula to writing treatments and it is important to take an approach that, without being overly tricksy, best suits the particular project and allows the writer's voice to come through. Don't be intimidated by the fact that this is a prose document – people in the industry know that you are a screenwriter and not (necessarily) a novelist, and the treatment will be judged primarily on the strength and dramatic potential of the idea and not on the beauty of the writing. On the other hand, take pains to avoid irritating the reader by scrupulously checking spelling, grammar and punctuation.

Test read

Friends aren't often very useful critics of screenplays, but they can be an invaluable resource for test reading treatments. Ask them to read it and then really listen to what they say, especially the bit after the obligatory, 'I thought it was really great...' Quiz them to see if they understand the story you think you have written and, if they don't, acknowledge that it is probably not that they are stupid but that you have not made it clear.

Treatments are an important part of the writing process and the development industry, and must be given the time and thought required to make them both fit for purpose and as good as the writer can make them.

6. A CAREER IN SCRIPT DEVELOPMENT

INTRODUCTION

When the process of script development succeeds it is the most enjoyable and satisfying experience. Discussing stories with other creative people is an education and endlessly fascinating and feels like a huge privilege. Of course, script development may often be unsuccessful and disappointing. This chapter describes the nature of script development and offers some guidance on how to best ensure the development is a successful process.

The main problem with the 'job' of script development is that it isn't written down anywhere. There is no fixed description that sets out the process or the boundaries of development work, or any useful document to refer to that can help guide us through the different scenarios we may encounter. There is no list of probable or possible situations and how best to navigate them, and often, to cap it all, lots of us 'fall' unprepared into the role of script developer. Though we may approach the task responsibly, if we are not clear about demarcating the roles and boundaries it may prove to be a very stressful and difficult process.

To be clear, my definition of script development is the process by which the developer works with a writer on a project with the intention of making the script better placed for the next stage, i.e. finding a producer, seeking an agent, making an application for funding, or production of the film itself. The script developer will be anyone who works on the script who is not the writer. This could be another writer, or a producer, or a director, or a script developer who may be attached to the production or the production company, the funding body or working freelance.

A developer may have started out as a producer (though often styled 'creative producer' rather than 'developer'). Coming to development via producing usually means that the developer has completed at least one project such as a short film, television content or a feature film. The process of reading a story idea and then seeing it go through the various development stages to reach the screen is a very sharp and useful education in story development.

The other route to script development is to be good at script reports. Readers who write reports that are useful and valued sufficiently by either the writer or the producer become script developers when one or both ask the reader to do more detailed, face-to-face work.

DEVELOPMENT MEETINGS

The transition from writing script reports or producing content to running development meetings is a major one and should not be underestimated. Producing becomes driven by largely practical considerations and reading scripts and writing script reports is a task requiring skills in analysis and the understanding of the potential and the problems of the proposed project. The process of script development, however, is all about the writer; the developer has to productively assist the writer achieve the best potential that exists in the written script. This is the most important task of the developer, and the developer's biggest responsibility is to create a working climate in which the writer may produce the best possible work.

The two important maxims of the development process are: (1) writing is re-writing, and (2) in rewriting, nothing is sacred. Developers have to hone and perfect two interpersonal skills to do this job well – the ability to listen and the ability to communicate clearly, as the development process is guided through meetings.

Preparation

When meeting a writer for the first time, here are some points to bear in mind. First, make sure you have enough time between receiving the script and the meeting date to prepare. Find out about the background to the project: is this the first draft or has the project already been through stages of development? If so, don't ask for earlier drafts or previous scripts, but, if a short document exists that articulates the central idea, try to obtain it. Find out the origins of the project: is it the writer's original idea, or the producer's? Or is it an adaptation? The answers will affect the way you approach the material. Writers will have a very different relationship to their own stories, as opposed to having being hired to do the writing.

If the story is adapted and you are not familiar with the original, you need not necessarily read, watch or research the source material. Your contribution to the process is in assessing the project as a piece of film, and knowledge of the source may be a distraction. Do research the writer, however, and find what else they have written, and read or watch it.

The script

It is essential to read the script in one sitting so as to get a sense of the whole story. Most scripts you read will remind you of other films, and you should note these as they may be a useful topic during a meeting with the writer. If the story appears to conform to a genre that you are not especially familiar with (kids' films, westerns, sci-fi, war films) find time to watch classics of the genre. A second reading of the script will always be worthwhile and ensure more accuracy in your notes and thinking. Remember to note good elements – a well-written character, a beautifully crafted image – as well as your reservations.

The meeting

Prepare, and, if possible, memorise, the points that you believe are pertinent to the script you have read, but be flexible enough to respond to what the writer says at your meeting.

The heart of the problem in any script may often be connected with the relationship between the premise, the structure, the characters and the genre. Anyone who reads a script will be able to offer an opinion about whether or not they like it. What characterises a good developer is in offering the writer a way of understanding why and how elements of the script may not be working well. This is not the same as knowing and giving the writer the answers. In fact, try not to provide your answers because that is what the writer has to do. The developer needs to concentrate on knowing and pointing out why there is a problem. The purpose of the meeting is not to tell the writer what may not work or how to fix it, but to hold the discussion that will allow them to make the useful connections for themselves.

Breaking the ice

Do not omit to catch up with where the writer is by the time you meet; since your reading the draft, the writer has probably thought a lot more about the script and has often done further writing. Be sure to find out what work the writer thinks is required. If the writer has also noted something that you have (e.g. 'I am struggling with the structure; I am not sure where the first act should end...') then open the discussion there. If the writer doesn't suggest any ways to work on the script that they have considered, then it's up to you to raise your most important point.

Always outline possibilities in a value-free way but don't expect immediate responses. It takes time to absorb and process change but a good writer will do so. Asking the writer what, precisely, they want the audience to feel at certain points is a good way to begin the discussion. You will be in a good position to describe the way your feelings were engaged by the script and your response should be valued by the writer. Finally, it is important to remember when writing meeting notes that they are a plan for the meeting only; you can't plan for the development of the project – the object of the meeting is to assist the writer to do this.

Genre

Using genre as a framework for your discussion is one of the best ways to help the writer see why certain elements in the script are unsatisfactory. Referring to films that you and/or the writer see as belonging to the same genre as the script is an invaluable aid to establishing areas of agreement. This can produce an agreed way of discussing why elements of the script do and don't work within the generic conventions. It is, of course, important not to be prescriptive. The developer's job is to confirm the genre the writer is following and, where two or more genres may be cited, to discuss the story in the light of the conventions of both genres.

Origin of the story

Finding out from the writer of the script where the original idea came from may be useful but not of primary importance. Often the origin of the story and the story in the script may differ. A long account of the inspiration for the idea may have very little to do with your assessment of the problems that need to be discussed. But, if you are trying to establish what matters most to the writer, enquiring about the original idea may be revealing, not just for what is important to the writer but, equally, for what is not.

THE DEVELOPER'S APPROACH

Negative reactions

Negative reactions to a script are more common than we may care to admit. It is absolutely essential that a developer does not arrive at a meeting feeling angry about the way the writer has represented some character or some topic (homeless people, or the middle classes, or dolphin-watching voyages). In particular, do not indicate how tedious and boring you found reading the script.

The fact that someone has worked to complete a draft script is assurance that it has importance and matters to them. Your job is to discover this key to the script and, as far as possible, to nurture it. All the other decisions about the events and the structure of the story, which characters are needed, who they are and how they are characterised, and where and when the story is set, should be open to question. Your job is to make sure the best choices have been made to serve that original and essential inspiration.

Developer's experiences

One approach that works well in the developer's relationship with the writer is for the developer to relate a personal experience that chimes well with the events or the themes in the script. This can strengthen the enthusiasm and trust between developer and writer.

This happens at moments that begin with, 'You know what? Something like that happened to me. I walked in on a conversation that I wasn't meant to hear...' Or, 'I missed a ferry on a Greek island and had to find someone to take me in...'

Basically, this involves giving something of yourself that is personal and human. You can't plan this, and it can't be forced, but don't be fearful if it just happens. It is a good thing.

Flexibility

The main purpose of the meeting is to agree the priorities for the next stage. Although you go to the meeting being clear about what you consider needs attention first, it is important to keep your mind open to what comes up in the meeting – it may just be that something the writer says unlocks a big problem and becomes clearly the best thing to do next.

If you have been given formal requirements for the development process, these must, of course, be observed; but, if you have the freedom, it may be more useful to go on to produce an outline or a treatment rather than a full redraft as the next stage.

There are many different ways of communicating. If you are meeting with someone who doesn't say much don't panic about filling the silence. Similarly, if the writer doesn't pause for breath, lob in questions that will slow them down so you can maintain your place in the process. Don't allow the conversation to get sidetracked into discussion about particular scenes; if this is happening, steer the conversation to much more general things as it will be more productive in the end.

WRITERS

Writer-directors

There are lots of apparent problems in a script that can be resolved with a camera and an edit suite but it is hard to disguise a lack of truthfulness in the premise, or a main character whose actions are implausible.At the beginning of a meeting with a writer-director make it clear that the job of development is to get the story right. The director and producer will make the latter-stage changes to the script to get it ready to be filmed and this will be made far easier if the development has been carried out really well.

Co-writers

It is important with co-writers to spend a bit of time finding out how they work together – literally who does the typing, how often they can get together, when did they meet, have they done other projects together. If both are equally inspired and committed it shouldn't make any difference if you have one or two writers in the meeting.

THE NEXT STAGE

The meeting ends with a reiteration of the agreed priorities for the next stage of the development process. If the priorities are as you anticipated in your preparation, all well and good, but if some other issue arose at the meeting (or even subsequently), make sure you note it for when you meet again, which may be some time later. Deadlines must be precise and jointly agreed and you should confirm whether or not your brief allows you to be available to the writer for further discussion. From the developer's point of view, it would be unfriendly to say, 'Don't speak to me until we next meet in January.' The developer should be in a position to offer to clarify points or discuss possibilities that occur to the writer. The situation to avoid is having the writer use you as a 'permission person' or as a distraction from progressing the development. The writer should leave the meeting absolutely clear about what to do next.

Once a script is in development it is possible to enter a situation where the developer has to steer the project between the various, and often competing, demands of the team involved in it.

To do this the developer needs to know what the competing demands are. Typically, an actor has a fixed and limited window in which he or she can read the script, but the writer or director is still not happy with the draft; or the producer wants to bring in a new or additional writer; or the director has quite a different approach to the story-world from the writer. There is no easy way to calm such troubled waters but the developer is well placed in these situations to negotiate and offer solutions, effectively working for everyone, the developer's only priority being the script.

Another important role of the developer is to champion the project and the writer to the people and organisations who may enable the film to be produced. The developer needs to be able to talk skilfully about both the writer and the project in a way that excites interest. Many writers may find it hard to speak (as opposed to write) about themselves or their project in an interesting way. One reason for this is that the writer has been working on the idea, if not the script, for years, and the original simplicity of its meaning has been lost. Writers will commonly enthuse over their latest addition to the script, which, out of the context of the last draft, appears nonsensical.

Another reason to do this, though, is to gain the respect of the industry so that your opinions are trusted. Good developers are hard to find, and building a little reputation, just one good producer who really values what you think, will raise your own standing and that of development in general. This also holds true when you are talking about films. It is really important not to express negativity or hate them. If they didn't work for you, use your skills to figure out what was missing, or why it was boring, and talk analytically rather than critically.

It is common to hear new writers talk about development hell. In fact, this term refers to the point when a script is put into 'turnaround', i.e.the script is available, but encumbered by the prior development costs. However, the term is used by writers to mean that they are struggling!

It is a very valuable experience for a writer to have a script in development, and, however difficult it seems, to describe the process as hell is wrong. Of course, if it wasn't so difficult, everyone would write film scripts. The writer's responsibility in the development process is to consider all suggestions with an open mind; to respect the experience that is being offered and not to be negative.

Developers should never overinvest in a project; it's not your job to lie awake worrying about a script problem, or to email every thought you have about it, or to research everything there is to know on kidnapping in Russia, or cotton-picking in the deep South. And you certainly don't have to mourn the end of a project if it doesn't go into production. Most projects don't! It is still a really fun, creative, demanding and rewarding job if you can balance your levels of involvement well.

Finally...

A couple of years ago I was running a workshop with the Israel Film Fund and one evening our group went to a Bedouin settlement in the heart of the West Bank to a makeshift cinema for a screening of a film called *The Lemon Tree*. This tells a simple story about a Palestinian widow, Salma, whose lemon orchard has become a sniper security risk to the new Israeli Defence Minister, who has moved into a new home behind it, and the order is given to cut the orchard down. Salma takes on the might of the Israeli government to challenge the decision and, in the process, has an affair with her young, handsome lawyer. At the screening there were five young Palestinian village girls, maybe 14 or 15 years old who, I was told, had never seen a film before. As it began they went quiet, and didn't move a muscle as they watched the character assert her human and moral rights, and express her sexuality with passion. I don't know what the girls were thinking and feeling but they were completely engaged and I am certain they will never forget that experience and how something significant changed for them that day.

Film is such a powerful storytelling medium. Our privileged access in the West means we may catch a nap or check our emails during a screening, and it is really shocking and humbling to be reminded that it matters.

The aim of this book is to help improve the quality of screenplays available internationally, quite simply because all our stories matter.

SELECTED ONLINE RESOURCES

SCRIPTS ONLINE

www.simplyscripts.com – Extensive database of scripts and transcripts of feature films, both produced and un-produced, available to view and print. Collates its library from a number of online databases so covers scripts from classics like *Chinatown* to the latest releases such as *Minority Report*. Clearly states if it is a shooting script or transcript and occasionally holds early drafts of new classics such as *Three Kings* and *American Beauty*. There are sections specifically for TV and radio scripts and a good links section.

www.script-o-rama.com – If you want to know more about writing screenplays you can download your favourites here. This is a real film fan site and does much of the trawling for you for the latest and most authentic scripts for films from Hollywood to cult classics.

www.iscriptdb.com – Large movie script database. The site also contains a database of screenwriters and interviews with screenwriters. Prides itself on being the first to have many scripts online and has a section dedicated to screenwriters reviewing the latest scripts doing the rounds of Hollywood.

www.zoetrope.com – The Virtual Studio section of this website is a submission destination and collaboration tool for filmmakers – a community where artists can submit and workshop original work and where producers can make movies using built-in production tools. Membership is free but you have to sign up before gaining access to the virtual development section and area dedicated to new screenwriters.

www.triggerstreet.com – New site and offshoot of Kevin Spacey and Dana Brunetti's Triggerstreet production company. If scripts get into the site's top 10 they automatically enter into a 90-day first-look agreement with Triggerstreet. Good source of reviewing unproduced scripts

TREATMENTS

www.writingtreatments.com – Articles, samples, advice on writing treatments.

SALES SITES

Below are the addresses for a selection of script sale sites. Essentially these are platforms for new writers to present their scripts to industry executives.

www.praxisfilm.com
www.thesource.com.au
www.screenscripts.com/browsing.htm
www.scriptsales.com

REFERENCE SITES

www.bfi.org.uk – An enormous site that contains information about British Film Institute services and through its Film Links Gateway provides useful lists of organisations, libraries, script sites and competitions.

www.writersguild.org.uk – The Writers Guild of Great Britain – the main guild for established writers whose website includes interviews and advice.

www.scriptfactory.co.uk – The Script Factory's own site includes information about what we do, with details of training, events and development services, plus event transcripts, FAQs and other useful resources.

www.industrialscripts.co.uk – Courses, resources and networking site of this London based company.

www.ukfilmcouncil.org.uk – The UK Film Council was the Government-backed strategic agency for film in the UK. It was closed in April 2011 but still retains a useful website with links to other UK organisations.

www.launchingfilms.com – The web site for the FDA, and the Guide Book to download includes an essential monthly guide to theatrical releases as well as Home Entertainment.

www.screendaily.com – Online version of the trade magazine.

www.imdb.com – Essential search engine for credit info.

www.boxofficemojo.com – Stats heaven giving: opening weekends, number of screens, production budget, marketing budget, distributor, domestic (US), international and worldwide totals... all this AND an overseas breakdown. Could it get any better? Great tool for getting the populist view on what people are watching and where.

www.bbc.co.uk/writersroom – Mini-site from the BBC focusing on writing for the screen. Useful for tracking what competitions and funding are available to new writers as well as words of wisdom and encouragement from writers working for the screen today.

ONLINE NETWORKING

www.shootingpeople.org – Shooting People's daily Filmmakers and Screenwriters Network and weekly Script Pitch list. You can join these email networks to get news, views and information about screenwriting and filmmaking, and have the opportunity to ask questions and pitch projects.

www.bbc.co.uk/filmnetwork – An off-shoot from the BBC main site focusing on new filmmaking. Focus is on shorts but gives a good overview of schemes, screenings and events happening in the UK.

UK FILM MARKET OVERVIEW AND TRENDS

There is a series of handbooks published annually that provides a year-on-year analysis of the film industry in the UK exposing broad trends in the growth and make-up of the market.

British Video Association Yearbook – obviously now including BluRay. The handbook itself is extraordinarily expensive, though invaluable, giving the year-on-year performance of each of the entertainment windows (theatrical, ppv, video buy, video rental, BluRay and satellite broadcast) as well as a breakdown of trends in terms of audience make-up, genre, age, etc. The BVA website at **www.bva.org.uk** also contains some really useful material (stats, opinion, etc) to help towards understating this market.

The Film Distributors' Association – The trade body for distributors has an excellent website at **www.launchingfilms.com** which is an essential resource from the perspective of exhibitors and distributors alike. Available on request is an annual report, plus yearbook and various essays/statistical analysis. Excellent!

Screen Digest – **www.screendigest.com** – an international website that collates media reports. Used mainly by the media industry, most of the reports are for sale. However, it does have a database of free articles and research from different territories. Useful in terms of giving insight into what the hot topics of the day are and also for looking at future threats and opportunities facing the film industry.

CAVIAR Report (Cinema and Video Audience Research) – This annual report is funded by exhibitors to provide a comprehensive demographic breakdown of the cinema-going audience and trends in cinema viewing to potential advertisers. In terms of giving audience analysis it is the bible but it is very much a service which the industry pays for and access comes at a premium. That said, sample PDFs giving recent top-line information on audience trends is available on the business site connected to Pearl & Dean: **http://business.pearlanddean.com**

UK Film Council – UKFC has until this coming year produced an annual statistical yearbook – in 2010 this was published as a fully digital and searchable website for the first time. It offers the most comprehensive and accessible picture of film anywhere in the UK, and it can be found at **http://SY10.ukfilmcouncil.ry.com**. Obviously, with the demise of the UKFC, this may not be replaced in future years – but we presume that some sort of stats will be available from the new-look BFI.

Cinema Exhibitors' Association – **www.cinemauk.org.uk** – includes an annual report that gives overall figures for number of screens, admissions, gross box-office takings, revenue per admission and revenue per screen.

BOX OFFICE

Box Office Glossary

The main source of immediate and accessible box-office performance figures is always going to be the topline given in *Screen International*. These figures consist of a series of top 15/10/5 charts for the last weekend and can give a good indication of how a film currently showing is performing on the circuit. Always beware, though, of taking exhibition performance as indicative of how a title will eventually fare. Many that are slow performers at the box office or quick to drop out of the charts can more than make up in the home entertainment window and there are many sleeper titles such as *My Big Fat Greek Wedding* that can loiter below the radar of the top 10 for weeks accumulating a good box-office return before exploding on to the chart.

Terminology

Week: The number of weeks a film has been on release.

Three/Four/etc day gross: The weekend takings for a particular territory.

Screens: The number of screens the title is showing on.

Screen Average: The average amount taken per screen. This is a good indicator of how well a title is filling theatres. By averaging out the takings per screen this also evens out the playing field between small and large films by looking at performance rather than just the gross figures.

Seven-day % change: This indicates the rate at which a film's audience is dropping off. As soon as a film opens there is a natural drop off as it saturates its market and uses up its 'must-see' potential. Percentage change is also a good indicator of what type of word of mouth a film is getting. A film that is getting good word of mouth will tend to have a smaller % change and, in some cases, a small film with low P&A but good word of mouth can actually see its % change go up.

Total Gross: This is the total amount that the title has taken in that territory since its release.

There are numerous sites which give accurate box-office info though most have a North American bias. If reading statistics in chart form gives you a headache, it's definitely worth subscribing to Charles Gant's excellent box-office blog in the *Guardian*, giving a weekly analysis of the weekend's UK box-office results in a beautiful prose roundup: http://www.guardian.co.uk/film/series/at-the-british-box-office

Otherwise some of the better stats sites include:

Screen International – www.screendaily.com/box-office
EDI – www.acnielsenedi.com
The Hollywood Reporter – www.hollywoodreporter.com
Box Office Report – www.boxoffice.com
Box Office Guru – www.boxofficeguru.com
Internet Movie Database – www.imdb.com
Box Office Mojo – www.boxofficemojo.com
Variety – www.variety.com/Home

RELEASE SCHEDULES

www.launchingfilms.com/cgi-bin/releases.pl – FDA website gives a month-by-month breakdown for the next six months of scheduled theatrical releases in the UK collating release and box-office information.

Screen International – www.screendaily.com – Production Focus provides post-production listings from which to predict upcoming UK films.

www.imdbpro.com – A pay-to-subscribe section of the well-known website. It has all the depth of the traditional site but is more industry focused giving extensive coverage of: films currently shooting, release schedules, box-office analysis on films past and present, business news, and a festival news and calendar section.

Subscription is currently £40 a month but there is a free two-week trial if you would like to explore.

FESTIVALS

www.screendaily.com – A yearly calendar of festivals is available online and a yearly festival diary is given away with *Screen International* in January which is always worth keeping hold of.

www.filmfestivals.com – Handy if overly complicated site detailing what's what in the world of film festivals.

www.londonscreenwritersfestival.com – The site of the London Screenwriters Festival held annually in October.

SCRIPT FACTORY PROGRAMMES

For information about the next dates or to book a course for your organisation or company please visit **www.scriptfactory.co.uk**

INDUSTRY SCRIPT READING

Whether writing coverage for a producer or funding body, or offering feedback to a writer, the analysis of the script is the same while the style and delivery of each report is specific. Using The Script Factory's structured approach to screenplay analysis, this one-day course explores the key principles of writing script reports, includes a comprehensive guide to current work opportunities, and offers individual feedback on your chosen style of practice report.

Course Outline

Prior to the course, participants will be given an un-produced feature film script to read in preparation.

Teaching sessions include:

- Overview of a reader's role in the current UK industry.
- The responsibilities of a good reader – how to keep informed about the film market in order to offer accurate analysis.
- Distilling and assessing the core film idea. Great scripts start with a great idea, we'll consider what elements are essential for a strong film story and we'll practise defining the core dramatic premise of a film and writing appropriate loglines.
- Mastering the art of writing synopses.
- Assessing the story: how to analyse genre and structure.
- Analysing screenwriting skill: can this writer create screenworthy characters and craft compelling scenes?
- Finding work as reader: who to approach, how to sell your skill.

After the course, all participants will have the opportunity to read a second script and prepare a report on which they will receive individual feedback from the course tutor.

WRESTLING THE REDRAFT: PRACTICAL SCRIPT DEVELOPMENT

It's true what they say: writing is re-writing. Good script development is the single most important task for writers, developers and producers but is still the area with the least clarity about its processes. A solid understanding of screenwriting theory is essential but translating that theory into practice is not always straightforward. Each movie project raises its own unique set of challenges - of course, that's why it's fun, but it can also be frustrating and can sometimes feel like you're moving backwards. Having worked in active international development for over 10 years, with both experienced and emerging writers, Script Factory directors Lucy Scher and Justine Hart have devised a brand new programme that comprehensively examines the potential problems and explores how to navigate through the tricky development process, avoiding the common pitfalls and setting the next draft on course to exploit all the potential strengths of a movie idea.

This two-day course is primarily aimed at script developers, readers and producers. However, if you are a writer with a script that hasn't yet been optioned then this course contains valuable tools for analysing and improving your own work.

Course Outline

This is a highly practical course, using material that is currently in development. Prior to the course participants will be given a first draft of a script to read along with an accompanying reader's report. Overnight, between the two teaching days, a second draft of the script will be read.

DAY ONE

Session 1: Development Roles.

This introductory session examines the role of a developer within the creative process, including how to manage the expectations of producers, funders and directors. Primarily, however, we will consider how to establish the most positive dynamic between developer and writer with the aim of empowering the writer to produce the best work they possibly can.

Session 2: Analysing the material: We're writing a movie.

The initial stages of development are all about finding the best movie in the material. We'll lay out an approach for determining whether the key elements of the story are in place and whether the current draft is exploiting the strongest aspects of the idea. Most attention will be given to how the story aims to engage the audience: what does the story mean? does this ring true to a current cinema audience? how are we invited to care about the characters and the outcome?

Session 3: The first meeting

This session looks at how to approach the first development meeting; gaining the writer's trust; understanding the story the writer wants to tell and why; prioritising feedback to keep the next stage of development focussed.

Session 4: Development notes and the writers' next steps.

Too much feedback (however intelligent and constructive) can be counter-productive; this session considers how to write development notes that don't overwhelm the writer but that provide a useful resource for addressing the next stage of development. We consider how to adapt your style to suit the way each writer works and explore how to offer ongoing support between drafts. In this session we'll consider useful documents to work on between full re-drafts such as treatments, outlines, first act rewrites.

Overnight participants will be invited to read a second draft of a script and prepare feedback to the writer.

DAY TWO

Session 1: One step forward, two steps back?

What do you do if the next draft has got worse? How do you respond when the writer has taken a completely different direction to the one discussed in your development meetings? In this practical session we'll consider how to respond to a second (and third and fourth!) draft by the same writer: how to keep everyone in the process positive even when progress is apparently slow; how to ensure that the next draft doesn't repeat the same problems; how to help the writer achieve clarity about the project when the woods are in the way of the trees.

The remaining sessions on Day 2 aim to tackle the nitty-gritty of script development issues:

Session 2: Characters to serve the story.

Has the writer created the best characters to serve the story? Do we care about those we're supposed to in the way the writer intended? Are there enough characters or too many to serve the story? Writers spend months with their characters often resulting in characters who are too complex or contradictory for an audience who will only spend a hundred minutes getting to know them; a key job for the developer is often to help the writer simplify the journey of the main character without feeling that they have compromised on truthfulness. Conversely, how do you help a writer flesh out an underdeveloped character?

Session 3: The second act blues.

Developers generally prove their worth most when it comes to dealing with the structure of the story. In this session we'll give particular attention to the second act and ensuring that it remains focused on the dramatic question. Are there clear turning points that reinforce why we are watching this story? Do the stakes build convincingly? Is there the right balance between character development and plot? What else needs to be layered into the idea in order to ensure that there is sufficient material to keep the second act interesting?

Session 4: Honing the craft.

Development cannot and does not aspire to replace writing talent, however screenwriting has very specific craft techniques that can be learnt and that aren't necessarily natural to the writing process. This final session aims to ensure that developers are equipped with a thorough understanding of the key craft techniques in order to help writers give depth, texture and professionalism to their work.

WRITERS' WORKOUT

A chance to write and put theory into immediate practice. This hugely popular workshop course for writers is designed to strengthen your screenwriting skills and is ideal for those who have already completed a draft and are looking for inspiration to address the re-write or to create the next project.

Talent can't be taught, and storytelling is an instinctive skill, but screenwriting is *a craft* and the more you practise any craft the better you will get.

Pretty much everyone in the film industry will tell you that a good screenplay depends on a strong story idea and certainly even the very best writing can't hide a weak story. But, going beyond 'story', what makes a screenplay sparkle is the detail: well observed characters rendered immediately through one distinct action; clever exposition that implies a credible history but keeps us firmly rooted in the present; dialogue that aches with the burden of what it's concealing; beautiful imagery that defines the emotional landscape of the film; surprising moments that resound with truth.

Screenwriting is a precise and economic craft. Each scene and each exchange of dialogue should define character, be full of drama, come layered with subtext and resonate with meaning. Whilst a focus on getting the story right is essential, a satisfying screen story can only be written with a solid understanding of the nitty-gritty of screenwriting craft. Of course, the more practised you are in screenwriting craft then the more efficient you will be at solving story problems and generating fresh material that is worthy of the big screen.

Writers' Workout is a practical two-day course designed to consider some of the essential techniques that are unique to the screenwriting form. Participants will be trained in key principles and coached through a series of practical exercises designed to stretch your creativity, hone your technique and send you back to your screenplay with renewed enthusiasm and sharper instincts.

Working in small groups with a high tutor/student ratio, some of the work you do will be specific to your current screenplay but much of it is designed to equip you with skills and approaches that can be applied to both current and future projects.

DAY ONE
Beyond the obvious
Interesting drama rarely happens in coffee shops but a disproportionate number of screenplay scenes seem be set in them. This first session is about freeing up your creativity, adding life and texture to your script by avoiding the obvious choices of scenes and settings and discovering the drama that might lurk off the beaten track.

Characters: don't I know you from somewhere?
Continuing the theme of breaking from the obvious, this session thinks about how to build original screen characters. We will consider how to introduce your characters and establish their histories without falling into awkward exposition. We'll look at creating drama in the gap between what your characters choose to reveal and the truths they are concealing (even from themselves). And we'll also think about the personal habits and behavioural tics that make a screen character unique, memorable and recognisably 'human'.

Breaking rituals
The best way to get to know someone is by what they do. Everyone has their rituals whether it's the way they take their coffee, the rented holiday home they return to each year, or the section they choose first from the Sunday papers. This session uses practical exercises to explore what happens when those rituals are broken and considers how a shift in behaviour can be used effectively to convey significant changes in a character's circumstance or attitude.

Opening images
First impressions count! The opening images of a film should prime the audience for the story that is to follow, encapsulating the main story idea and setting the tone. This session looks at how to flag up themes and introduce characters in a way that is appropriate to the kind of film you are writing - be it a high concept genre movie or a multi-strand art house drama.

Overnight homework

Between the first and second day writers will be required to complete an overnight writing exercise related to your current screenplay idea. This will be discussed with your tutor and fellow group members on the second day.

DAY TWO

Group Feedback

The second day starts with an opportunity to discuss the writing exercise and get constructive feedback from your tutor and fellow writers.

Point of View

Some film stories, such as 21 Grams or Magnolia, make a particular structural feature of exploring narratives from different points of view. Of course, all storytelling is subjective, its meaning derived from whose perspective we are asked to interpret events. A skillful manipulation of point of view is crucial to the screenwriter's job: it's how you keep us aligned with your chosen protagonist, ensure that subplots remain relevant to the central storyline, establish dramatic irony and generate tension right up until the final pages of script. In this session we will consider the impact of choices regarding point of view, including decisions about the overall story design as well as methods of ensuring that we experience the emotional impact of each scene as you, the writer, intend.

Dialogue

In life we rarely ever say directly what we mean (or even if we do, our words get twisted and the person we're speaking to thinks that we meant something else!). In screenwriting, it's always what remains unsaid that is so much more important and the ability to layer dialogue with an unspoken subtext is a fundamental screenwriting skill. This session will provide plenty of practice at doing just that, as well as ensuring that dialogue exchanges serve as actions and reactions which move the story on.

Scene breakdowns

The only way to become fluent in the language of screenwriting is to study as many screenplays as possible. This course, like all Script Factory programmes, is designed to encourage writers to actively analyse screenwriting texts and learn about story structure, scene function and character arcs by breaking down the inner workings of a successful script.

Only by analysing a screenplay, beat by beat, can we really appreciate how rich and textured this writing form is. In this final session we will look at how to compile a scene breakdown, both as an essential learning tool and as a useful method of developing your own story.

This course is limited to just 8 participants.
It is taught by Lucy Scher, one of The Script Factory's directors.

STORY DESIGN

A two-day screenwriting workshop aimed to help you work an idea for a film into a solid screen story.

Storytelling is a talent. However, skillful film storytelling requires more than just natural creativity: screenwriters need to learn how to shape a story into one that can be told over 90 odd minutes, keep an audience rooted to the screen for the duration and ensure that everyone is emotionally engaged with the plight of the characters as the story unfolds.

Taught by Lucy Scher and Rob Ritchie, this 2-day workshop considers the essential elements of designing a story for the screen. Whether you're working at the idea stage or you're in the process of redrafting, this programme aims to help you ensure that your idea is achieving its fullest potential. Will your story speak to the widest possible audience? Are you using the best cinematic devices to hook the audience in? Have you created a compelling and intriguing story world? Are the characters that populate your story the best ones to serve the idea?

DAY ONE
Defining the Universal Conflict
Screenplays are about specific characters in a specific situation. The films with the most enduring appeal, however, are those that allow the audience to recognise the characters' problems and predicaments and relate them to their own experience. This opening session explores how to find the universal conflict in a dramatic idea so the audience is personally engaged in what's at stake.

Framing the Story: Beginnings and Endings

An audience needs to know *why* they are watching a film and to leave the cinema satisfied that there was a purpose to the story being told. What is it they are supposed to care about? What ending will the story and the audience demand? This session illustrates how to open your story with a clear dramatic question and create an ending that has real impact and meaning.

Cinematic Hooks

Continuing the theme of how to begin your screenplay, this session explores how to give ideas for dramas the big screen treatment by using recognisable hooks from cinematic genres. The session also illustrates how to create external drama to reveal the most intimate internal character journey.

Locations and Story Worlds

In some films the setting of the story is a character in its own right, in others the location is merely a backdrop. Whether it's the domestic interiors of melodrama or the epic landscapes of action-adventure, the mise-en-scene is the source of the images and metaphors that give the story its meaning. This session examines how choosing the right locations can both clarify the meaning and liberate the cinematic potential of a story.

DAY TWO

What do you want from me?: Matching Characters and Story Types

The way an audience relates to character depends on the kind of story being told. Everyone loves an underdog, but not necessarily in an action-adventure film. The heroines of romantic comedies may not believe that they are worthy of true love but the audience certainly needs to think that they are. This session aims to dispel some myths about what makes a 'good screen character' and considers how to make certain your protagonist has the right attributes for their role.

And what do you do exactly?: Secondary Characters

Story design naturally concentrates on the fortunes of the protagonist - the character the story is all about. But how do the secondary characters - the hero's allies and adversaries - fit into the overall design? This session looks at how identifying the dramatic arc of each character in a screenplay can help to solve problems of plot and structure.

Building a Sequence

Screenplays are routinely discussed in terms of Acts and Scenes. While this allows the main beats of the story to be analysed it obscures the fact that movies are composed of sequences. This session explores story design by illustrating how a sequence is built and addresses the question: how many sequences does it take to make a screenplay?

Story Re-design

This final session aims to leave you equipped to approach your story idea with fresh eyes and offers some useful tools for the continuing development of your screenplay.

SCREENWRITING UK

A screenplay-writing course designed specifically for writers who are working on a first draft film script but have yet to break into the film industry.

It's a long way from the computer screen to the big screen, and it takes talent, determination and more than a decent break to get there. The Script Factory has devoted over a decade to working in the gap between new writers and the film industry, supporting writers through the early stages of their career and helping the industry identify and nurture new talent. Screenwriting is, of course, an artistic endeavour but a screenplay is also a product for an industry. Essential to success is an understanding of how the UK film industry works, how a script reader or producer determines the potential of a film idea and an awareness of the script development process.

This two-day screenwriting course combines in-depth teaching on the principles of good screenwriting and invaluable insider knowledge from working writers and producers. It's designed to provide participants with the understanding they need to turn a strong idea into a well-crafted screenplay that has the potential to attract interest from producers, developers and funders.

DAY ONE
Stories & Genre

This first session considers the universal function of storytelling and examines how cinema audiences recognise and respond to different story types. Confusion over story type or genre is often cited as one of the key reasons why screenplays are rejected. A pile-up in a thriller may add to the excitement, yet a car-crash in a drama might be devastating. An understanding of the subtle (and not so subtle!) distinctions between genres is critical to managing the audience's emotional response to the events on the screen. By considering the expectations inherent to each genre, we will begin to consider how to develop a screenplay that offers the reader a meaningful and satisfying story experience.

Premise & Conflict

Whether it's about saving the world or growing up, the success of every screenplay depends on the clarity and strength of the dramatic conflict. This session explores the kinds of problems that a screen character might face and considers how to ensure that the story is invested with enough potential conflict to sustain the tension for the duration of a feature film.

Screenplay Structure

A brilliant screenplay is one that keeps a reader turning the pages from beginning to end and tells that reader that the audience will be glued to the screen for every moment of the film that follows. This session explores the basic principles of structuring a screen story from getting the audience hooked to delivering a satisfying ending.

DAY TWO
Character Journeys

Whether you start off with a dramatic concept and then find characters to dramatise it through or you start with characters and build a story around them, it is ultimately the journey your characters take which defines what your story is. However, different story types require different character arcs – some characters will be forever transformed, some will learn a lesson, others will get their chance to show what they are really made of and a few will simply grow up. This session interrogates what we mean by character change and how you can build convincing character change into your story.

The Controlling Idea
Take a lesson from *Shaun of the Dead*

Films, like all stories, have a cultural function: to communicate something to an audience that helps them to understand themselves better, or to make sense of the world. The meaning we take away from watching the film is called the Controlling Idea. This session explores how to identify or determine the controlling idea of a story and how to use this a tool when developing the screenplay.

Treatments, Pitching and The Development Process
This final session explores the development process from sending out the first draft to receiving feedback and planning a rewrite. We will also offer helpful approaches to preparing treatments and a simple guide to preparing a pitch.

Course Tutors
The course is taught by two of The Script Factory's directors Lucy Scher and Justine Hart.

kamera BOOKS

ESSENTIAL READING FOR ANYONE INTERESTED IN FILM AND POPULAR CULTURE

Tackling a wide range of subjects from prominent directors, popular genres and current trends through to cult films, national cinemas and film concepts and theories. Kamera Books come complete with complementary DVDs packed with additional material, including feature films, shorts, documentaries and interviews.

Silent Cinema
Brian J. Robb

A handy guide to the art of cinema's silent years in Hollywood and across the globe.

978-1-904048-63-3 **£9.99**

Dalí, Surrealism and Cinema
Elliott H. King

This book surveys the full range of Dalí's eccentric activities with(in) the cinema.

978-1-904048-90-9 **£9.99**

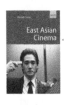

East Asian Cinema
David Carter

An ideal reference work on all the major directors, with details of their films.

978-1-904048-68-8 **£9.99**

David Lynch
Colin Odell & Michelle Le Blanc

Examines Lynch's entire works, considering the themes, motifs and stories behind his incredible films.

978-1-84243-225-9 **£9.99**

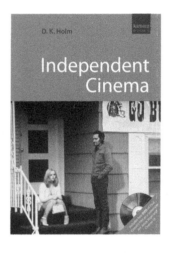

→ Accompanying DVD features
Paul Cronin's *Film as a
Subversive Art: Amos Vogel
and Cinema 16*, a documentary
profile about the founder of
the New York Film Festival and
America's most important film
society

→ Includes previously
unpublished interviews with
Jill Sprecher (*Clockwatchers*),
James Mangold (*Walk the Line*)
and Guy Maddin (*The Saddest
Music in the World*)

Independent Cinema
D. K. Holm

D. K. Holm aims to define a term all too carelessly used both by media
commentators and marketers, and distinguish it from categories such
as avant-garde, underground, experimental or 'art' films, with which it is
often confused.

By contrasting studio-era Hollywood with changes in the business
since the 1970s, and the rise of companies such as Miramax and New
Line, it shows the birth of a commercial environment in which the new
independent cinema can emerge.

Profiles of specific filmmakers such as Guy Maddin, Jill Sprecher and
James Mangold suggest how diverse personalities use independent
cinema for individual ends.

978-1-904048-70-1   £9.99